Navigating the Digital Transformation Imperative

ICT Integration, Deployment & Global Competitiveness

By

Carl Roberts

Copyright

ISBN:978-1-5356-0325-6 (eBook)
ISBN:978-1-5356-0326-3 (Paperback)
ISBN:978-1-5356-0328-7 (Hardcover)

Library of Congress Control Number:
2025921984

Dedication

I dedicate this book to my granddaughter Rhianna, and children: Heston, Bradford, Zachary, and my only daughter Gabriella, who at the time of writing this dedication is an MD on rotation at Brooklyn, NY hospitals. She is a graduate of the St. George's University (SGU) doctor of medicine program based in pure Grenada.

I further dedicate this book to the people of Grenada, and St. Vincent and the Grenadines for giving me the permission to engage IT project managers in the government and businesses. You provided me with the opportunity to collect very important data for analysis that, as presented in my doctoral research study and within the pages of this book, may deliver pathways to improved socio-technical developmental solutions.

The ideas, concepts, techniques and strategies for designing, developing, governing and maintaining processes for the integration and deployment of ICT, are part of my legacy. This book also applies succinctly to the wider Caribbean region, other CARICOM countries, and the 'developing world.'

The support of everyone aided substantially towards the success of my first book. Lastly, I dedicate this book to my close friends and associates who have impacted or encouraged my successful attempt at becoming an author.

Acknowledgement

I wish to express my sincere gratitude and appreciation to a team of professional writers and publishers who managed this project. My first book collaboration was overseen by Karl Baushman, head of publishing and marketing, Ken Williams and Jim Xaviour who led the project at different stages of the process. Robert Green assisted in this important venture to create a manuscript that reflects the literary insights from my doctoral research study. The goal was to create pleasurable reading along with a sense of purpose and urgency to execute solutions.

My deepest respect is extended to the wonderful people of St. Vincent and the Grenadines, for welcoming me with open arms to conduct research for my doctoral study. It is the basis of this literary effort. My greatest admiration, love, and respect to my peace-loving brothers and sisters of my birth country, Pure Grenada, the Spice Isle of the Caribbean. The major portion of data used for my research study was collected in Grenada. It was my utmost pleasure interacting with all the IT project managers/participants who signed up for my interview from both countries.

I salute the brilliant minds of our young academicians and future leaders, enthusiastic pace setters of the digital culture shift, landscape, industry, and our most important assets; people. They have a tremendous responsibility and duty to fulfill. The projections for a digital economy and robust information society are only possible through a trained and skilled workforce capable of utilizing cutting edge technology and achieving sustainable development goals. This venture may demand mastering every qubit of intelligence assistance and diligence to be successful.

Sincere thanks to all my friends who I communicated with about my intentions and ideas to write this book, including Dr. Zorina Frederick and my life-long friend Dr. Sonia Nixon, MPH. The topics discussed and your encouragement was absolutely meaningful. I extend my gratitude for the knowledge you shared. I also extend special thanks to my partner Lyma Dunbar and DJ Code Red for a great job promoting the pre-launch, and implementing a post-launch marketing strategy highlighting the book on social media 'Reels' and their weekly radio program. The video trailer was aired every Saturday from 12:00pm to 2:00pm on 'ThePeoplesChatRoom.com,' a Caribbean infused talk show that tackles today's topics as we pay tribute to our community.

Please join us on Saturdays@12:00pm with the following link for live programing via YouTube: https://www.youtube.com/@ThePeoplesChatRoom.
'iChunesRadio.com' is our powerbase, with simulcast on 'Cultural Vibrations Radio' (cvr247.com) and rebroadcast at 12:30 pm every Sunday on 'IslandBeatRadio.net.' Your deep insights, ideas, concepts, and exceptional level of work provided the jump-start to market this classic, and kept it alive publicly.

Preface

The desire to write a book of this magnitude and significance commenced after graduating with a terminal degree in Information Technology (IT). My curiosity for its core subject of Information and communication technology (ICT) was a no brainer. Due to the research study I conducted in the Caribbean, a greater understanding of how the potential for ICT may be leveraged for social and technical development was triggered. The various manifestations of computerization efforts pursued by organizations and governments of the countries I visited left an enormous impression.

The concept of standardization became relevant as similarities emerged even if the scope of what I interpreted as individual goals seemed uneven. Although my observation hinted the realization of quite similar agendas, the differences in management approaches captured motives against a backdrop where the deployment of development processes had consequences. I also knew that the bigger, longer term milestone of individual sacrifices for national goals was only one side of the coin. Project success and sustainability at this early stage means a whole lot more.

This book offers an expert exploration of the digital shift currently unfolding, with a dedicated focus on the unique opportunities and challenges within the Caribbean region. Readers will acquire the real, actionable strategies that drive successful ICT adoption and deployment, learning how to dramatically lower barriers to innovation, e-commerce, and online e-learning. This is more than a technical manual; it is a resource designed to foster innovation and create tangible pathways for growth.

Education plays a pivotal role in shaping cultural change and digital transformation. It is critically important for reforms in the schools' curricula and the education system as a whole to synchronize with the digital transformation agenda. A new approach to teaching should replace antiquated colonial systems. That being said, I wrote this book with a purpose and intent to assist students at all levels of academia, technology researchers, business professionals, IT practitioners, and Caribbean governments to circumvent the perilous next forty years of a digital divide or the technology gap with the developed world.

Table of Content

Introduction

The Digital Transformation Imperative in the Eastern Caribbean

Across the Eastern Caribbean, digital transformation is no longer a distant or optional goal—it has become an urgent and strategic imperative. The region's long-term economic resilience, social equity, and global competitiveness fundamentally depend on its ability to effectively embrace, integrate, and leverage Information and Communication Technologies (ICTs). As detailed in the research conducted by Carl S. Roberts, ICTs present a powerful and transformative pathway for economic development by enhancing public service delivery, fostering business innovation, and expanding educational access. Despite this tremendous potential, the transition to a fully digital society within the Eastern Caribbean remains constrained by a complex web of structural, strategic, and infrastructural challenges that must be carefully addressed to realize technology's full benefits.

One of the region's most pressing contextual realities is its pronounced vulnerability to natural disasters, particularly hurricanes, which regularly threaten lives, infrastructure, and economic stability. This vulnerability accentuates the critical need for robust, adaptive, and resilient digital infrastructure capable of withstanding and rapidly recovering from climate-induced shocks. With the increasing frequency and severity of natural disasters driven by climate change, digital resilience is rapidly emerging as a foundational pillar of sustainable development in the Caribbean. Governments, private sector actors, and regional organizations are thus prioritizing investments not only in expanding connectivity but also in ensuring that digital platforms, data centers, and communication networks can remain operational—or be quickly restored—in the face of environmental disruptions.

Supporting this urgency, institutions including the Inter-American Development Bank (IDB) emphasize that the long-term prosperity and competitiveness of Latin America and the Caribbean hinge significantly on how effectively these regions can incorporate cutting-edge digital technologies such as artificial intelligence (AI), cloud computing, big data analytics, blockchain, and the Internet of Things (IoT) into their economic systems and social infrastructures. The strategic integration of these emerging technologies promises to accelerate innovation, optimize public administration, enhance disaster risk management, and open new avenues for entrepreneurship and employment.

Yet, despite these promising avenues, the reality of ICT project implementation in the Caribbean is sobering. Project failure rates remain alarmingly high, with studies indicating that up to 85% of IT development initiatives across the region are classified as either complete or partial failures. Such failures manifest through projects that exceed budgets, face significant delays, deliver limited functionality, or fail to achieve intended social and economic impacts.

Several critical factors contribute to these disappointing outcomes. Many ICT projects suffer from the absence of clearly articulated strategies that link technology adoption to broader development objectives. Inadequate stakeholder engagement often leads to insufficient buy-in and mismatch between project designs and user needs. Furthermore, budgetary support for digital initiatives is frequently insufficient or inconsistently prioritized, undermining proper implementation, capacity building, and sustainability efforts. Institutional readiness—reflected in weak governance frameworks, fragmented coordination mechanisms, and limited skilled human resources—presents an additional barrier that hampers effective project planning, execution, and monitoring.

The stakes could not be higher. Failure to successfully integrate ICTs into the public and private sectors risks deepening the Caribbean's marginalization in a rapidly digitizing global economy. Without strategic, well-executed digital transformation, Caribbean nations may struggle to compete in emerging markets, attract investment, foster innovation ecosystems, and improve the quality of life for their citizens.

In conclusion, the Eastern Caribbean sits at a crossroads: it can choose to invest comprehensively in strengthening digital infrastructure, governance, and skills or risk falling further behind. Overcoming the multifaceted challenges impeding ICT project success requires coordinated efforts across government, private sector, academia, civil society, and international partners. The future prosperity of the region depends on the ability of all stakeholders to learn from past shortcomings, adopt tailored strategies, and collaboratively build a resilient, inclusive, and innovation-driven digital economy.

Why ICT Integration Matters for Development and Global Competitiveness

In developing countries, and particularly in the small island nations of the Eastern Caribbean, ICTs represent more than just a tool—they are a catalyst for transformation. The integration of ICTs into public services, education, and commerce can increase transparency, improve the quality of life, and promote inclusive economic growth. Digital solutions are central to enabling e-government services, facilitating mobile learning (m-learning), and fostering the development of e-commerce platforms that can connect local businesses to global markets.

At the societal level, ICTs have the power to reduce inequality by extending opportunities for education, employment, and social participation to historically marginalized communities, including those in rural and underserved areas. Access to high-speed internet, for instance, allows individuals to engage in remote work, participate in online learning, and access telemedicine—all crucial elements for resilience in times of crisis, such as during the COVID-19 pandemic.

From a developmental lens, the successful integration of ICTs can help Caribbean nations overcome structural disadvantages associated with small market size, limited natural resources, and geographical fragmentation. By investing in digital infrastructure and capabilities, these countries can leapfrog traditional industrial stages and position themselves as agile, knowledge-based economies.

Yet, the process of integration is complex. It demands not only the adoption of new technologies but also a fundamental rethinking of organizational processes, institutional cultures, and policy frameworks. As Roberts' study illustrates, ICT integration must be underpinned by strategic planning, cross-sector collaboration, and robust implementation frameworks that align with local contexts and capabilities.

Overview of the Book's Purpose, Audience, and Structure

This book draws from a comprehensive qualitative study to explore the strategies employed by Information Technology (IT) project managers in the Eastern Caribbean to integrate ICTs effectively. Grounded in the Technology Acceptance Model (TAM), the book examines the factors that influence technology adoption, particularly perceived usefulness and perceived ease of use. Through multiple case studies conducted in Grenada and St. Vincent and the Grenadines, the research uncovers actionable insights into the challenges and enablers of successful ICT integration in both the public and private sectors.

The primary audience for this book includes policymakers, IT professionals, project managers, development practitioners, and scholars interested in digital transformation in developing regions. It also speaks to international donors, educators, and business leaders seeking to understand the practical realities of ICT deployment in small island states.

The book is structured around three key themes that emerged from the research:

1. **Organizational Structures and Leadership** – Exploring how internal management systems, governance, and stakeholder dynamics influence ICT project outcomes.
2. **Infrastructure and Strategic Implementation** – Investigating the role of network development, such as government-wide area networks (GWANs), in enabling digital services across sectors.
3. **Budgeting, Buy-in, and Institutional Challenges** – Highlighting the financial, cultural, and operational barriers to ICT adoption and strategies for overcoming them.

Additionally, the book includes chapters on the theoretical foundations of technology acceptance, implications for professional practice, and recommendations for policymakers and practitioners aiming to drive meaningful digital transformation.

A Personal Anecdote to Engage Readers

The journey that led to this research is deeply personal and rooted in my own experience navigating the digital landscape of the Caribbean. I was born in St. George's, Grenada, and resided at my parents' home on Williamson

Rd. Raised in a household that valued education, discipline, and the free flow of ideas, I was shaped by my mother, a dedicated educator and headmistress of St. Paul's Model School, who inspired in me a lifelong commitment to knowledge and community development. My father, a World War II veteran, taught me the importance of communication and the disciplined pursuit of excellence.

At the age of 17, my dad introduced me to AM radio—a medium of electronics and electrical engineering science that transmits Amplitude Modulation signals, carrying voice and music onto a radio signal (wave) and then sends that signal to distant places. My first job was as a Technical Operator at the Government of Grenada AM radio station. One of the more important aspects of my job was to bring the world news to the population. At specific times during the day, it was my responsibility to tune the receiver in the control room via a patch panel to receive the world news relayed from the BBC News Service and the Voice of America, which I then transmitted to the country daily.

During the nation's 1979 historic revolution, which installed Comrade Maurice Bishop as the new revolutionary prime minister, I was promoted to on-air announcer and engaged in activities such as live DJ entertainment, other program initiatives, and news reporting. After a few years, I transitioned to become an innovative collaborator with my older brother, whose goal of pioneering the first legitimate FM radio station (SpiceCapitalRadio) soon became a reality. We were issued the first FM license to operate legally, setting the precedent for approximately fifteen other FM radio stations operating today.

After migrating to the USA in 1983, I pursued computer network applications, hardware, and software through self-education, and later an in-depth understanding of systems as my ultimate challenge. The rest is history.

Growing up in a region where technological resources were often scarce, I developed a keen awareness of the disparities in access and opportunity that digital divides can create. I remember sitting in classrooms with outdated equipment and limited internet access, watching as other parts of the world surged ahead in digital innovation. Yet, I also saw the resilience and ingenuity of Caribbean communities—educators using personal funds to purchase school supplies, civil servants innovating with limited tools, and local entrepreneurs finding creative ways to bring their businesses online.

These early experiences fueled my passion for exploring how ICTs could be leveraged to uplift Caribbean societies. As I advanced in my career in information technology, I became increasingly aware of the systemic challenges that impede progress: fragmented strategies, inadequate training, misaligned policies, and the absence of unified implementation frameworks.

This book is a culmination of my academic and professional efforts to address these challenges. It is both a scholarly contribution and a call to action for Caribbean leaders and global partners to invest in the digital transformation of the region—not merely through technology acquisition, but through the development of human capital, institutional capacity, and inclusive governance structures.

I have had the privilege of engaging with IT project managers who, despite limited resources and complex environments, have demonstrated remarkable innovation and dedication. Their stories, insights, and strategies form the backbone of this book. Through their experiences, we gain a deeper understanding of what it takes to succeed in ICT integration in the Eastern Caribbean—and what lessons might apply to other developing contexts around the world.

Chapter 1

Understanding the Eastern Caribbean Context

Socio-Economic Landscape and Digital Readiness

The Eastern Caribbean region, comprised of small island developing states (SIDS) such as Grenada and St. Vincent and the Grenadines, is marked by distinct socio-economic and developmental characteristics that both define and constrain its trajectory. These countries face a unique set of structural challenges stemming from their geographic isolation, relatively small landmass and populations, limited economies of scale, and heavy dependence on vulnerable sectors like tourism and agriculture. These factors, compounded by the frequent occurrence of natural disasters—particularly hurricanes—pose persistent obstacles to robust, sustainable development and global economic competitiveness.

As of 2020, the population of Grenada was approximately 112,523 people, while St. Vincent and the Grenadines was home to roughly 110,940 residents. These populations present moderate to high population densities, with about 331 individuals per square kilometer in Grenada and 285 in St. Vincent and the Grenadines. Such demographic profiles reflect tightly-knit, urbanized societies where social cohesion tends to be strong. However, these small and dense populations also strain existing infrastructure and limit the scalability of development projects. The small domestic markets restrict the diversity and size of labor pools and reduce national revenue collection, thereby constraining public investment capacity, particularly in areas requiring significant financial outlay such as advanced digital technologies and infrastructure.

Historically, the economic models of these Eastern Caribbean SIDS have relied heavily on tourism, agriculture, and limited manufacturing activities, which placed them in vulnerable positions due to external shocks like global market fluctuations, climate change, and natural disasters. In recognition of these limitations, the governments of Grenada and St. Vincent and the Grenadines, along with regional bodies, have increasingly identified information and communication technologies (ICTs) as indispensable tools for economic diversification, resilience building, and social development. ICT presents opportunities to leapfrog traditional development stages by enhancing public sector efficiency, fostering innovation in the private sector, expanding educational access, improving healthcare delivery, and facilitating greater socio-economic inclusion.

Despite widespread acknowledgment of ICT's transformative potential, digital readiness within the region remains uneven and underdeveloped. Both Grenada and St. Vincent and the Grenadines have made commendable efforts to create enabling environments through the formulation of national ICT policies and their active participation in regional programs such as the Caribbean

Regional Communications Infrastructure Program (CARCIP) and the Eastern Caribbean Regional Improvement Project (EGRIP). Grenada's Digi4R initiative, for instance, aims to digitize government registries and back-office processes, reflecting a strategic focus on improving administrative efficiency and transparency.

In St. Vincent and the Grenadines, several targeted ICT projects have been launched, including the Electronic Document and Records Management System (E-DRMS), Public Key Infrastructure (PKI) application for enhanced cybersecurity and electronic authentication, and the Intelligent Bus Management and Monitoring System intended to improve public transportation services. These initiatives provide tangible case studies for comparison and learning within the region. However, despite these advances, the deployment of ICT solutions remains somewhat fragmented and sporadic. Challenges such as limited workforce training in digital competencies, insufficient change management frameworks, and the lack of systematic adoption of globally recognized project management and architectural methodologies—like the Project Management Body of Knowledge (PMBOK) and The Open Group Architecture Framework (TOGAF)—have led to inefficiencies and inconsistent outcomes in the implementation phase.

Nevertheless, significant progress is evident in building the foundational digital infrastructure necessary for sustainable development. CARCIP-funded projects in Grenada have facilitated the rollout of high-speed broadband internet across key regions, thereby enhancing connectivity and laying the groundwork for future digital services. Collaboration between governments and private telecommunications providers, notably companies like Digicel, has also played a crucial role in expanding internet coverage, improving service reliability, and reducing connectivity costs for the population.

Education remains a critical frontier in the region's digital transformation journey. Ministries of education across the Caribbean, including those in Grenada and St. Vincent and the Grenadines, have initiated ICT integration strategies aimed at modernizing teaching and learning environments. Pilot programs have introduced computer labs, interactive digital learning platforms, and national digital content development initiatives to improve educational quality and access. Yet, these efforts face significant implementation barriers, including inadequate teacher training and readiness, insufficient hardware and software resources, inconsistent ICT policies, and infrastructural gaps, particularly in rural or underserved communities. Greater emphasis on mobile learning (m-learning) technologies offers a promising avenue to bridge these gaps by leveraging widespread mobile phone penetration to extend educational resources beyond traditional classroom settings.

Despite existing challenges, the momentum toward comprehensive digital readiness in the Eastern Caribbean is steadily increasing. This progress is propelled by an urgent regional imperative to diversify economic activities, strengthen resilience against external shocks, and promote inclusive growth. The adoption of digital services has already facilitated the establishment of online platforms for tax payment, business registration, and e-banking, creating a preliminary digital ecosystem conducive to broader e-government service delivery and the development of vibrant digital commerce environments.

If current initiatives are accelerated and coherently aligned—through improved governance, capacity building, sustainable investment, and the institutionalization of best practices in ICT project management—the Eastern Caribbean stands poised to capitalize on digital technologies as a foundation for inclusive and dynamic socio-economic development. This evolution holds the promise of transforming the region's traditional vulnerabilities into strengths, fostering greater connectivity, innovation, and opportunities for its citizens in an increasingly digital global economy.

Unique Challenges and Opportunities for ICT Adoption in the Region

ICT adoption in the Eastern Caribbean region is shaped by a complex interplay of persistent constraints and emerging opportunities. On one side of the spectrum, high project failure rates pose a critical challenge that undermines confidence in digital transformation efforts and stalls momentum. Empirical research concerning developing countries, including those in the Caribbean, reveals sobering statistics: only about 15% of ICT projects achieve their intended success, while 35% fail outright, and the remaining 50% deliver only partial outcomes. These figures underscore systemic barriers embedded across multiple levels of governance and implementation, ranging from inadequate project planning and technical capacity gaps to institutional resistance and fragmented institutional frameworks.

A fundamental obstacle is the widespread absence of standardized and formalized IT deployment frameworks within national public sector institutions. Rather than adopting internationally recognized project management methodologies and architectural standards, many government agencies continue to rely on informal processes entrenched in traditional administrative habits. These ad hoc approaches often result in fractured project execution, leading to a misalignment between the realized outcomes of ICT projects and the broader national development objectives they aim to support. Moreover, the lack of consistent and rigorous mechanisms for monitoring, evaluation, and feedback exacerbates inefficiencies, rendering it difficult to learn from past experiences or to ensure accountability.

Organizational resistance to change constitutes another significant impediment to effective ICT adoption. Within the public sector, digital literacy levels among employees and decision-makers frequently lag behind the pace of technological advancements. This digital skills gap fosters apprehension and skepticism towards new ICT initiatives. Fear manifests in several dimensions—fear of job redundancy due to automation, fear of increased scrutiny arising from transparency-enhancing technologies, and a general discomfort with adopting unfamiliar tools and processes. These attitudinal barriers often prove more challenging to overcome than technical difficulties, as insufficient emphasis on change management strategies and stakeholder engagement leads to diminished buy-in and low utilization of implemented systems.

Budgetary constraints compound these issues further, despite broad recognition of ICT's transformative potential. Many Eastern Caribbean governments grapple with limited fiscal space, resulting in funding that is often inadequate, delayed, or inefficiently allocated to digital projects. Consequently, ICT initiatives frequently suffer from fragmented implementation, obsolete or incompatible hardware, and an inability to advance beyond experimental pilot stages. Even when international development partners or donor agencies provide grants or concessional loans, the constrained absorptive capacities and weak governance mechanisms within beneficiary countries limit the effective disbursement and productive use of such capital. This gap between funding availability and utilization underscores the urgent need to build institutional capacities for financial and programmatic management of ICT investments.

Policy coherence and enforcement remain recurring challenges that hinder systematic progress. Although most countries in the region have developed national ICT policies, e-government strategies, and related regulatory frameworks, these documents often remain unapproved by legislative bodies or Cabinet, quickly become outdated, or are implemented in a fragmented manner due to weak institutional mandates. Without clear, enforceable, and harmonized policy guidance, project managers operate without strategic alignment, frequently making decisions based on individual interpretations rather than coordinated, cross-sectoral approaches. This siloed policy environment limits inter-agency collaboration and hampers efforts to build integrated digital ecosystems that span multiple ministries and public entities.

Despite these formidable challenges, several promising factors present significant opportunities for accelerating ICT adoption in the Eastern Caribbean. The relatively small population sizes and centralized governance structures of nations such as Grenada and St. Vincent and the Grenadines create a conducive environment for piloting, refining, and scaling up digital solutions at a national and even regional level. Regional initiatives like the Eastern Caribbean Regional Improvement Project (EGRIP) have demonstrated success in promoting interoperable e-government platforms, including shared electronic tax filing systems, digital identification schemes, and procurement portals, showcasing the benefits of coordinated, regionally harmonized technology applications.

Importantly, the region's demographic profile features a substantial youth population that is increasingly digitally savvy and widely connected through mobile devices. This youthful cohort has driven burgeoning interest and growth in digital services such as mobile banking, e-learning platforms, and digital entrepreneurship. Young business owners and innovators, operating in both urban centers and rural communities, harness ICT tools to access broader global markets, generate employment opportunities, and offer innovative digital products and services. This demographic dividend represents a vital asset for the region's ICT-driven transformation agenda.

E-government initiatives offer significant scope to improve public sector efficiency, reduce corruption, and enhance citizen satisfaction. By migrating crucial government services—such as business licensing, tax compliance, and procurement—to online platforms, governments can streamline administrative processes, reduce face-to-face interactions that sometimes foster corrupt practices, and increase operational transparency. Recognizing these benefits, regional governments are gradually adopting digital tools for internal operations including human resource management systems, electronic document handling, and enhanced communication networks.

Beyond governance, ICT adoption has begun to positively impact key socio-economic sectors critical to the Eastern Caribbean's development. In healthcare, the introduction of electronic health records, telemedicine services, and mobile health (mHealth) applications offers promising avenues to improve access to quality medical care, particularly in remote or underserved locations. The agricultural sector is also embracing digital innovations, leveraging platforms that facilitate greater market access, provide accurate weather forecasting, and optimize supply chain logistics, thereby boosting productivity and resilience. Tourism, which remains the backbone of many island economies, stands to benefit enormously from enhanced digital marketing strategies, online booking systems, and virtual customer engagement platforms that broaden its global reach and competitiveness.

However, these technological advancements need to be accompanied by substantial institutional reforms to be truly effective. The successful adoption and utilization of ICTs depend not merely on technology deployment but on strengthening IT governance frameworks, building capacity among public sector employees, and establishing robust accountability systems for project design and implementation. These endeavors must be framed within localized strategies that carefully consider cultural contexts, current institutional capabilities, and national development priorities in order to be sustainable and impactful.

In summary, while the Eastern Caribbean faces significant barriers to ICT adoption—including high failure rates, organizational resistance, funding shortages, and policy incoherence—the potential opportunities afforded by demographic trends, regional collaboration, and sectoral applications provide an optimistic outlook. With a concerted emphasis on structured project management, capacity building, policy integration, and adaptive change management, the region can harness digital technologies to drive inclusive socio-economic development, improve governance, and build resilience against future challenges.

Key Stakeholders: Government, Private Sector, and Civil Society

The success of ICT integration in the Eastern Caribbean depends on the coordinated efforts of a diverse set of stakeholders, each playing a distinct yet interconnected role.

Government

Governments play a foundational and multifaceted role as the primary architects and drivers of national digital transformation. Their responsibilities encompass a wide range of critical areas, from the conception and formulation of comprehensive ICT policies and regulatory frameworks to the strategic investment in digital infrastructure and the active oversight of ICT project implementation across public institutions. Key ministries—particularly those responsible for information technology and communication, education, finance, and public administration—hold significant influence in shaping the national digital agenda and ensuring that ICT initiatives align with broader socio-economic development goals.

In the Eastern Caribbean context, governments have demonstrated increasing commitment to digital transformation through strategic, often large-scale programs such as the Caribbean Regional Communications Infrastructure Program (CARCIP), the Eastern Caribbean Regional Improvement Project (EGRIP), and Grenada's Digi4R initiative. These programs exemplify government-led efforts aimed at enhancing broadband connectivity, modernizing public service delivery, and improving the efficiency and transparency of administrative systems. Through such initiatives, governments seek to foster an enabling environment that promotes innovation, economic diversification, and citizen-centric service delivery.

However, despite the ambition and strategic intent behind these efforts, the effectiveness and sustainability of government-led digital transformation projects are frequently hampered by critical leadership gaps. A key challenge identified within public sector institutions is the prevalence of senior administrators and decision-makers who lack adequate technical expertise or digital literacy. This deficiency undermines their ability to critically evaluate ICT proposals, make informed decisions regarding budgeting and procurement, support technical teams, or effectively coordinate cross-departmental and inter-agency collaborations necessary for project success.

The absence of technical acumen among policy-makers and administrators can lead to misaligned priorities, underestimated resource requirements, and insufficient oversight, all of which increase the risk of project delays, cost overruns, or outright failure. For instance, procurement decisions may favor costly or unsuitable technologies, and monitoring mechanisms might be underdeveloped, resulting in poor accountability and limited learning from implementation challenges. This points to the urgent need for capacity building and digital literacy programs targeted not only at technical staff but especially at senior leadership within government, including ministers, permanent secretaries, and heads of agencies who shape ICT-related budgets and policies.

Leadership buy-in and active championing of ICT initiatives have proven to be among the most significant success factors in digital transformation efforts. When political and administrative leaders visibly support and advocate for digital projects, it fosters a culture of commitment, resource mobilization, and stakeholder engagement essential for meaningful progress. High-level sponsorship helps mitigate bureaucratic inertia, accelerates decision-making, and facilitates the alignment of multiple levels of government and development partners around common objectives. Conversely, projects lacking such high-level endorsement frequently suffer stagnation, poor resource allocation, and fragmented implementation, diminishing their impact and sustainability.

Moreover, effective government leadership in digital transformation entails more than just top-down support; it requires cultivating an enabling institutional environment that encourages innovation, accountability, and continuous learning. Strengthening digital leadership within the public sector must therefore become a central pillar of any ICT development strategy. This involves not only targeted training and skills development but also instituting governance frameworks that embed ICT strategy into the highest levels of government decision-making and promote collaboration across ministries, agencies, and external stakeholders.

In conclusion, while governments in the Eastern Caribbean have begun laying the groundwork for national digital transformation, bridging the leadership and capacity gaps—especially at the decision-making level—is critical to unlocking the full potential of ICT initiatives. Building strong, digitally literate, and visionary leadership teams capable of navigating the complexities of digital innovation will be instrumental in achieving sustainable, inclusive socio-economic progress through technology.

Private Sector

The private sector in the Eastern Caribbean plays a vital and multifaceted role in driving the region's digital transformation, serving both as a key service provider and a dynamic source of innovation. Telecommunications companies, with major players like Digicel at the forefront, are instrumental partners in the expansion of broadband internet access and in catalyzing public-private infrastructure investments. Through strategic collaborations with governments and regional organizations, these telecommunications firms have successfully extended internet coverage to underserved and remote communities, thereby fostering greater digital inclusion. Their efforts in enhancing mobile connectivity have empowered citizens and businesses alike, enabling greater participation in the digital economy.

Beyond the foundational role of connectivity provision, the private sector significantly contributes to technological innovation and digital service development across a variety of emerging fields. Sectors such as e-commerce, financial technology (fintech), mobile and web application development, and cloud computing services have seen heightened private sector activity and growth. Entrepreneurs, startups, and small and medium-sized enterprises (SMEs) increasingly recognize the transformative potential of digital tools to improve operational efficiency, reduce costs, expand market reach beyond local boundaries, and open new revenue streams. For example, fintech innovations have improved access to financial services by enabling digital payments, mobile wallets, and micro-lending solutions tailored to the local context.

However, despite these promising developments, the private sector faces a number of significant constraints that impede its full potential. High operational costs, including expensive internet tariffs and limited infrastructure in certain areas, present barriers to scaling digital ventures and achieving competitiveness. Additionally, the regulatory and legal environments often lag behind technological advancements. Weak or incomplete legal frameworks governing digital transactions, electronic signatures, data privacy, and consumer protection undermine business confidence and inhibit broader adoption of digital commerce. Furthermore, access to investment capital remains a persistent challenge for many innovative enterprises in the region. Local venture capital ecosystems are immature, and many SMEs struggle to secure affordable financing or attract impact investments targeted at early-stage digital startups.

To unlock the private sector's full innovative potential and support sustainable digital entrepreneurship, comprehensive policy reforms are urgently needed. Governments must prioritize the modernization of the digital finance landscape by developing clear regulations that facilitate secure online payments, digital lending, and other fintech services, while instituting robust cybersecurity protections to safeguard consumers and businesses alike from cyber threats. Strengthening intellectual property (IP) rights frameworks is equally essential to protect digital innovations and incentivize research and development within the region.

Beyond regulatory improvements, governments and development partners should increase investments in digital entrepreneurship ecosystems. This includes nurturing startup incubators and accelerators that provide critical mentorship, networking, technical assistance, and business development services tailored to digital enterprises. Access to seed funding and grants specifically targeted at fostering innovation and digital product development can also stimulate local talent and sustain emerging ventures. Public-private partnerships can play a crucial role in creating co-working spaces, innovation hubs, and digital skills training programs that enhance local capacities and foster a collaborative culture of innovation.

Encouragingly, some nascent programs and regional initiatives have begun addressing these needs, but scaling these interventions and ensuring their sustainability remain pressing priorities. A holistic approach that combines sound policy frameworks, targeted ecosystem investments, and collaborative stakeholder engagement will be instrumental in transforming the private sector into a powerful engine for digital transformation and economic growth in the Eastern Caribbean.

In conclusion, the private sector's dual role as a connectivity enabler and a driver of innovation is indispensable for the digital future of the region. By addressing existing regulatory, financial, and infrastructural challenges, and by fostering vibrant entrepreneurship ecosystems, governments can empower private companies—from telecommunications giants to small startups—to lead the charge towards a more inclusive, competitive, and digitally-driven economy.

Civil Society and Academia

Civil society organizations (CSOs)—including non-governmental organizations (NGOs), professional associations, faith-based groups, and community-based organizations—play a pivotal intermediary role between governments and citizens in the digital transformation process. These organizations often serve as important advocates for digital inclusion, ensuring that vulnerable and marginalized populations are not left behind in the rapidly evolving digital landscape. By focusing on empowering underserved communities, CSOs help bridge the digital divide through targeted outreach efforts such as ICT literacy training, awareness campaigns, and affordable access initiatives.

Beyond advocacy, civil society actors are instrumental in building digital skills at the grassroots level. Many NGOs and community organizations run ICT capacity-building programs that provide training in basic computer skills, internet navigation, and digital communication tools, enabling individuals to participate meaningfully in an increasingly digital economy and society. These grassroots training initiatives are particularly critical in rural and underserved areas where formal digital education infrastructure may be weak or nonexistent.

In addition, civil society organizations play a watchdog role by monitoring the fairness, transparency, and accountability of government ICT projects and digital initiatives. By providing independent oversight, conducting impact assessments, and engaging in constructive dialogue with authorities, CSOs help ensure that digital transformation initiatives adhere to principles of inclusivity, data privacy, and good governance. Their feedback and grassroots insights can be invaluable for shaping more responsive and participatory digital policies.

Parallel to the role of civil society, educational institutions—from primary and secondary schools to technical colleges and universities—are fundamental stakeholders in shaping the region's future digital workforce. These institutions have the responsibility to equip students with relevant digital skills, critical thinking abilities, and problem-solving competencies that are essential for success in digital economies. However, many educational institutions in the Eastern Caribbean face persistent structural challenges that hamper their ability to deliver contemporary digital education. These include outdated curricula that fail to keep pace with technological advances, insufficient professional development and training opportunities for educators to teach ICT effectively, and inadequate technological infrastructure such as limited access to computers, reliable internet, and modern software tools.

To overcome these challenges, governments must prioritize comprehensive investments in digital education infrastructure and resources. This entails not only upgrading hardware and connectivity in schools but also reforming curricula to integrate ICT across subjects and grade levels, ensuring students develop digital literacy as a core competency from an early age. Additionally, continuous professional development programs are essential to enhance teachers' digital skills and pedagogical approaches, enabling them to confidently incorporate technology into classroom instruction and facilitate active, student-centered learning environments.

Moreover, governments should promote lifelong learning initiatives that extend digital skills training beyond formal schooling to include adults, workers, and marginalized groups. Facilitating access to continuing education and vocational training in ICT-related fields through community colleges, online platforms, and workforce development programs will support ongoing digital inclusion and adaptable labor markets.

Academic institutions have a further critical role beyond direct education delivery: they serve as hubs for research, innovation, and policy development in the ICT domain. Universities and research centers in the region can contribute valuable evidence-based insights by conducting rigorous studies that assess the effectiveness of ICT integration efforts, evaluate digital readiness, and identify best practices tailored to the specific socio-economic contexts of Caribbean SIDS. Through pilot projects and experimental initiatives, academic institutions can test innovative digital solutions, provide proof-of-concept models, and generate localized data to inform more effective policymaking.

Engagement in national and regional forums, conferences, and collaborative networks enables academic stakeholders to share knowledge, influence digital policy discourse, and foster partnerships between government, industry, and civil society. Strengthening the linkages between academia and policy circles can help bridge gaps between theory and practice, ensuring that ICT strategies are grounded in robust research and adaptable to rapidly changing technologies and societal needs.

In summary, civil society organizations and educational institutions together form critical pillars of the Eastern Caribbean's digital ecosystem. By advocating for inclusivity, delivering essential skills training, monitoring digital governance, and generating evidence-based knowledge, these actors significantly advance the region's capacity to harness ICTs for sustainable and equitable development. For governments seeking to accelerate digital transformation, actively collaborating with and investing in these sectors is essential to build an empowered, digitally literate population prepared for the challenges and opportunities of the digital age.

International and Regional Organizations

International stakeholders—including multilateral development banks such as the World Bank and the Inter-American Development Bank (IDB), as well as various

United Nations (UN) agencies—play a crucial and multifaceted role in supporting digital transformation efforts across Eastern Caribbean countries. These organizations provide vital financial resources, technical expertise, and advisory services that enable small island developing states (SIDS) in the region to undertake complex ICT projects that might otherwise exceed their fiscal or technical capacities. Through grants, concessional loans, capacity-building programs, and policy advisory support, these international partners help bridge funding gaps, improve institutional capabilities, and accelerate the deployment of digital infrastructure.

Complementing the work of international donors and financiers are regional bodies such as the Caribbean Community (CARICOM), the Organisation of Eastern Caribbean States (OECS), and the Caribbean Telecommunications Union (CTU). These organizations serve as vital platforms for regional coordination, consultation, and policy harmonization in the digital domain. By fostering collaboration among member states, they facilitate knowledge-sharing, the exchange of best practices, and the development of consistent regulatory approaches that can enhance interoperability and reduce duplication of efforts.

One of the most important contributions of both international and regional entities lies in their capacity to harmonize standards, regulatory frameworks, and technical guidelines across borders. In a region characterized by many small, economically interconnected states, such harmonization is essential to enabling seamless digital services, regional data exchanges, and the creation of integrated digital markets. This collective approach allows individual countries to benefit from economies of scale, avoid regulatory fragmentation, and present a stronger, unified voice in global digital governance discussions.

Furthermore, these stakeholders actively fund and support cross-border projects that address regional infrastructure deficits and promote digital inclusion. Initiatives such as submarine fiber optic cables, shared e-government platforms, common cybersecurity protocols, and digitized customs and trade facilitation systems are often made possible through pooled funding and regional cooperation spearheaded by these organizations. This collective delivery model enables small island nations—each with limited domestic markets and resources—to "punch above their weight" in the global digital economy.

International and regional partners also play a critical advocacy role, championing digital inclusion and equitable access across the Eastern Caribbean. They emphasize the importance of addressing the "digital divide" by supporting initiatives targeting marginalized groups, rural communities, and vulnerable populations. Through technical assistance programs, policy dialogues, and funding mechanisms focused on inclusivity, they help incorporate digital equity considerations into national and regional development agendas.

Moreover, their involvement often brings global expertise and innovative solutions tailored to development contexts, such as low-cost connectivity technologies, digital skills curricula, and e-government frameworks adapted to SIDS. By leveraging decades of development experience and global networks, these stakeholders help Eastern Caribbean countries anticipate emerging technological trends and risks, positioning them to respond more effectively to future digital challenges.

In summary, the combined efforts of international and regional organizations are indispensable for the Eastern Caribbean's digital transformation journey. By mobilizing financial resources, fostering policy alignment, enhancing technical capacities, and promoting regional cooperation, these stakeholders enable small island states to overcome inherent structural limitations and collectively build resilient, inclusive, and competitive digital economies. Their sustained partnership with national governments and civil society is foundational to realizing the full social and economic benefits of ICT adoption across the region.

Conclusion

The Eastern Caribbean stands at a pivotal crossroads in its ongoing digital development journey. Despite enduring structural limitations—including geographic isolation, small domestic markets, and vulnerability to natural disasters—alongside ingrained resistance to change and significant capacity constraints within public and private sectors, there is an increasingly widespread recognition of the profound transformative potential that information and communication technologies (ICTs) hold for the region. This growing awareness is fostering a more optimistic and proactive environment for digital innovation and socio-economic advancement.

Several distinctive attributes of the Eastern Caribbean give the region unique advantages in harnessing ICT for inclusive growth. The relatively small size of its island nations allows for more agile decision-making and enables pilot projects and innovative solutions to be tested and scaled rapidly. Additionally, the region benefits from a youthful, increasingly digitally literate population with widespread access to mobile technologies, which serves as a dynamic catalyst for entrepreneurship and the emergence of new digital business models. These demographic and technological factors create fertile ground for vibrant digital ecosystems that can drive job creation, improve service delivery, and expand access to education and financial inclusion.

However, realizing this potential requires intentional and coordinated action that goes beyond technology deployment alone. A concerted effort must be made to nurture collaboration across the entire ecosystem of stakeholders—government entities, the private sector, civil society organizations, educational institutions, and international development partners. Only through such multisectoral partnership can the region effectively address persistent challenges such as infrastructure gaps, limited human capital, regulatory fragmentation, and societal apprehension towards digital transformation.

On the governance front, there is a critical need for strengthened leadership, enhanced digital literacy among policymakers, and the institutionalization of robust project management and accountability frameworks to ensure that digital initiatives are strategically aligned with national development objectives and are effectively executed and monitored. Investments in education must emphasize not only the modernization of curricula and teacher training but also lifelong learning opportunities that equip all segments of the population—including marginalized groups—with the digital skills essential for participation in the 21st-century economy.

Equity and inclusion must remain at the heart of digital transformation strategies to prevent the deepening of existing social divides. This includes prioritizing expanded affordable broadband access, particularly in rural and underserved communities, and designing e-government and digital services that are accessible, user-friendly, and responsive to diverse needs. Furthermore, supportive legal and regulatory reforms are necessary to foster trust, protect digital rights, stimulate private sector innovation, and create an enabling environment for startups and SMEs to thrive.

The road ahead for the Eastern Caribbean is undoubtedly complex, marked by risks as well as immense opportunity. It demands sustained political will, strategic investments, and a commitment to adaptive governance that embraces innovation and learning. By harnessing the collective strengths of its governments, private sector innovators, civil society advocates, and international collaborators, the region can overcome its developmental barriers and chart a resilient, inclusive, and sustainable pathway to digital transformation. In doing so, the Eastern Caribbean has the potential not only to enhance economic competitiveness but also to improve the quality of life for all its citizens, fostering a more connected, empowered, and prosperous society in the digital age.

Chapter 2

The Role of IT Project Managers

Who Are IT Project Managers in the Caribbean Context?

IT project managers in the Caribbean occupy a uniquely critical and multifaceted position within the region's rapidly evolving digital landscape. Unlike their counterparts in technologically mature economies, Caribbean IT project managers operate within a complex environment shaped by distinct economic, social, and infrastructural challenges. These professionals often serve as the linchpins that hold together intricate ICT initiatives, which are vital for bridging the digital divide, stimulating economic development, and modernizing both public and private sector operations across diverse island contexts.

According to Roberts (2020), IT project managers in the Eastern Caribbean mainly undertake leadership roles in ICT projects that support a broad range of national priorities, including government digital transformation efforts, business modernization initiatives, and educational reforms aimed at enhancing digital literacy and access. Their responsibilities extend well beyond traditional project management functions; they act as strategic facilitators who must effectively integrate technology into organizations often characterized by limited human and financial resources, entrenched bureaucratic processes, and varying degrees of technological readiness.

In many Caribbean countries, IT project managers are not only accountable for the technical delivery of projects—such as software development, network installations, or systems integration—but also for advocating the value of digital transformation within their organizations and across stakeholders. They frequently navigate a complicated socio-political terrain where competing interests, organizational silos, and shifting policy directives can affect project timelines and outcomes. This requires them to maintain a nuanced understanding of local governance structures, cultural norms, economic development priorities, and community expectations.

Moreover, Caribbean IT project managers often find themselves operating under significant constraints including limited access to modern infrastructure, budget limitations, and workforce capacity shortages. These challenges compel them to be innovative and resourceful, adapting global project management methodologies to fit local circumstances and leveraging available technologies in cost-effective ways. Their ability to coordinate efforts across multiple agencies, private sector partners, and international donors is essential for aligning project objectives with national development goals and achieving sustainable impact.

One of the most formidable challenges faced by IT project managers in the Caribbean is driving ICT adoption in environments where resistance to change is prevalent. Resistance can be fueled by fears of job loss through automation, prevalent digital illiteracy among staff, cultural skepticism toward unfamiliar technology, or dissatisfaction stemming from previous unsuccessful projects. Consequently, effective change management becomes a critical component of their role. These managers must skillfully deploy communication strategies, build stakeholder trust, foster participatory engagement, and provide capacity-building support to overcome apprehensions and ensure end-user buy-in.

Roberts' study highlights that IT project managers in the Caribbean come from diverse professional backgrounds—including computer science, business administration, information systems, and engineering—which equips them with a multidisciplinary skill set necessary to address the technical, managerial, and interpersonal dimensions of their work. This hybrid expertise enables them to understand complex technical requirements, apply project management best practices, and navigate organizational dynamics. Nevertheless, the rapidly evolving ICT landscape demands continuous professional development. These managers must regularly update their knowledge and skills by adopting emerging methodologies, software tools, frameworks such as Agile, PMBOK, or TOGAF, and integrating cybersecurity, data privacy, and cloud computing considerations into their project approaches.

Beyond project execution, Caribbean IT project managers contribute significantly to building institutional digital maturity by mentoring junior staff, advocating for stronger governance mechanisms, and supporting policy development that institutionalizes ICT best practices within government and private organizations. Their strategic leadership is instrumental in bridging gaps between technological possibilities and institutional realities, thereby accelerating the region's digital transformation journey.

In summary, IT project managers in the Caribbean are dynamic, resilient professionals who blend deep technical knowledge with strategic leadership and cultural sensitivity. They serve as essential agents of change, enabling their countries to navigate complex socio-technical landscapes and advance toward becoming digitally empowered societies. Strengthening their capacity and recognizing their pivotal role are critical steps toward harnessing the full benefits of ICT across the Caribbean region.

Critical Skills and Responsibilities

The success of IT projects in the Caribbean is closely tied to the competencies and effectiveness of IT project managers, who play a central role in orchestrating the planning, execution, and delivery of projects that are closely aligned with both organizational objectives and broader national development goals. Given the complex socio-economic and infrastructural landscape of the region, the demands on these managers extend beyond basic project oversight—they must possess a diverse set of technical, managerial, and interpersonal skills to navigate unique challenges and ensure sustainable impact.

Roberts (2020) provides an insightful analysis of the critical skills and core responsibilities that characterize the role of IT project managers in the Caribbean context. These competencies are essential for transforming the often high-risk and resource-constrained environment into a platform for successful ICT implementation. Understanding and strengthening these skills are vital not only for individual project success but also for advancing the region's overall digital transformation agenda. Key among these skills and responsibilities are:

1. Technical and Methodological Competence

IT project managers in the Caribbean must possess a deep and comprehensive understanding of recognized project management methodologies such as PMBOK (Project Management Body of Knowledge), Agile, and PRINCE2, adapting these global frameworks to the distinct socio-economic and infrastructural realities of the Caribbean context. Mastery of these established methodologies equips project managers with the tools required to structure projects effectively, manage scope, control timelines, allocate resources, and systematically identify and mitigate risks.

Beyond familiarity with these methodologies, competence in ICT-specific domains is essential. This includes a thorough knowledge of ICT systems architecture, the software development life cycle (SDLC), network and infrastructure deployment, cybersecurity principles, and data governance. Such technical proficiency ensures that managers can oversee the end-to-end lifecycle of IT projects—from initial requirements gathering, design, and development to testing, deployment, and ongoing maintenance—thereby guaranteeing the delivery of robust, scalable, and secure digital solutions.

Roberts (2020) highlights the critical importance of integrating dedicated IT implementation frameworks with broader project management methodologies to form customized hybrid approaches tailored to the Caribbean's unique environment. This integration recognizes that technology projects in the region often face challenges that are not fully addressed by standard methodologies alone—such as limited infrastructure, budgetary constraints, human resource gaps, and complex bureaucratic processes. By blending methodological rigor with contextual adaptation, project managers can develop flexible frameworks that maintain technical integrity while accommodating local organizational cultures, policy landscapes, and stakeholder dynamics.

For example, the Agile methodology's iterative and incremental approach may be particularly well-suited for ICT projects involving frequent stakeholder feedback and evolving requirements, whereas PMBOK's comprehensive structure supports governance and documentation rigor in public sector projects. PRINCE2, with its emphasis on defined roles and business justification, can aid managers navigating complex government procurement and accountability environments.

Moreover, IT project managers must be proficient in applying tools and software used for project tracking, documentation, risk management, and reporting—such as Microsoft Project, JIRA, Trello, or similar platforms—to facilitate transparency, real-time monitoring, and collaborative communication among dispersed teams and multiple stakeholders.

In practical terms, the capacity to tailor and integrate frameworks means project managers should continuously assess project conditions and stakeholder inputs, selecting or blending methodological elements to fit evolving project scopes and resource realities. They must also work collaboratively with technical teams, business analysts, and users to ensure that the chosen methodologies support effective requirements management, quality assurance, and timely delivery.

In summary, technical and methodological competence in Caribbean IT project management demands not only mastery of international best practices but also the skillful contextualization of these approaches. This synthesis enables project managers to deliver ICT projects that are technically robust, culturally appropriate, and operationally sustainable within the unique constraints and opportunities presented by the Caribbean environment.

2. Strategic Planning and Execution

Effective IT project managers are strategic thinkers who provide comprehensive oversight of the entire project lifecycle, guiding initiatives from their inception through careful planning, diligent execution, continuous monitoring, and formal closure. They are responsible for crafting detailed project plans that clearly define the project scope, identify and allocate necessary resources, establish realistic budgets, and implement robust risk management strategies. These foundational elements ensure projects proceed in a structured and disciplined manner, enhancing the likelihood of successful delivery within time and cost constraints.

In the Caribbean context, the role of strategic planning assumes even greater complexity and importance due to the region's unique economic, political, and infrastructural landscape. IT project managers must align their projects not only with organizational objectives but also with broader national digital agendas and international frameworks such as the Sustainable Development Goals (SDGs). This alignment ensures that technological investments contribute meaningfully to advancing socio-economic development, improving public services, and fostering inclusive growth across diverse island states.

A critical aspect of strategic planning in this environment involves the anticipation and mitigation of a wide range of potential obstacles that could derail project progress. For example, funding shortfalls are a frequent constraint faced by Caribbean governments and organizations. Project managers must therefore develop contingency plans that include phased implementation approaches, alternative financing strategies, or the prioritization of project components to ensure continuity in case of budgetary adjustments.

Political changes, including shifts in leadership or policy direction, can also impact digital initiatives. IT project managers must remain agile and politically astute, engaging with stakeholders across the political spectrum to maintain project support and adapt strategies as necessary to evolving governance contexts. This includes ensuring that projects maintain visibility, relevance, and alignment with the priorities of incoming administrations.

Infrastructural deficiencies—such as unreliable power supplies, limited broadband connectivity, and inadequate ICT hardware—pose additional strategic challenges. Project managers need to assess these risks early and incorporate mitigation measures such as selecting appropriate technologies that can operate in low-resource environments or developing partnerships with telecom providers to improve connectivity.

Moreover, effective strategic planning requires IT project managers to establish clear communication channels, foster stakeholder collaboration, and institutionalize monitoring and evaluation frameworks that provide real-time insights into project performance. This proactive approach enables early identification of issues and informed decision-making to keep projects on track.

In summary, strategic planning for IT projects in the Caribbean demands a holistic, forward-looking mindset that integrates technical project management best practices with an acute awareness of the local political, economic, and infrastructural realities. By anticipating risks, aligning with national and international development priorities, and embedding adaptive strategies, IT project managers play a pivotal role in delivering impactful digital solutions that drive sustainable socio-economic progress across the region.

3. Stakeholder Engagement and Communication

In the diverse and multifaceted environment of the Caribbean, effective stakeholder engagement and communication are essential competencies for IT project managers. Projects often involve a broad spectrum of stakeholders, including government officials and policymakers, private sector leaders, civil society and community representatives, technical teams, and end-users from various social and economic backgrounds. Each of these groups brings distinct perspectives, interests, and priorities to the table, making clear, inclusive, and adaptive communication indispensable to project success.

One of the primary challenges faced by IT project managers is bridging the gap between complex technical concepts and the non-technical understanding of many stakeholders. Managers must possess the skill to translate technical jargon, methodologies, and data into clear, accessible language tailored to different audiences. This helps demystify ICT projects and facilitates informed decision-making by ensuring that stakeholders fully comprehend project objectives, progress, benefits, and risks.

Roberts' research highlights the critical importance of maintaining continuous and meaningful stakeholder engagement throughout the entire project lifecycle—not merely during initial phases or formal presentations. Active engagement helps to build trust, foster collaboration, and cultivate a sense of shared ownership over ICT initiatives. This ongoing dialogue allows for the early identification of concerns, the incorporation of diverse feedback, and the adaptation of project approaches to better meet stakeholder needs.

To operationalize this, IT project managers often organize a range of participatory activities, including workshops, focus group discussions, stakeholder consultations, presentations, and regular feedback sessions. These forums serve as platforms for transparent communication, collective problem-solving, and consensus-building. For example, workshops can be used to co-create project requirements with end-users, ensuring that solutions are user-centric and contextually appropriate. Feedback mechanisms keep stakeholders informed on project developments and provide avenues for addressing challenges collaboratively.

Furthermore, effective communication strategies must be culturally sensitive and contextually relevant, respecting local languages, customs, and communication norms. In the Caribbean's multilingual and multicultural societies, tailored messaging and the use of multiple communication channels—including social media, community radio, and face-to-face meetings—can dramatically enhance reach and engagement.

Additionally, IT project managers should leverage digital collaboration tools and platforms that enable real-time information sharing and interactive communication among geographically dispersed stakeholders. This is particularly valuable for regional projects involving multiple nations or agencies.

In summary, stakeholder engagement and communication are not ancillary tasks but core strategic functions for IT project managers in the Caribbean. By fostering ongoing, transparent, and inclusive dialogue, these professionals can secure vital buy-in, mitigate resistance, enhance accountability, and sustain momentum throughout the project lifecycle. Building strong, trust-based relationships with diverse stakeholders ultimately lays the foundation for successful ICT adoption and lasting digital transformation in the region.

4. Leadership and Team Management

Managing multidisciplinary teams is a fundamental responsibility and cornerstone of effective IT project management in the Caribbean. IT project managers are tasked with leading diverse groups of professionals, including software developers, network engineers, business analysts, quality assurance specialists, and administrative personnel. These teams often operate across multiple locations— spanning different offices, islands, or even countries—adding layers of complexity to coordination, communication, and collaboration.

Effective leadership in this context requires not only technical oversight but also strong interpersonal and organizational skills. IT project managers must motivate and inspire team members by setting clear goals, recognizing individual and collective achievements, and fostering a positive and inclusive work environment. The ability to manage conflicts constructively is particularly important, as multidisciplinary teams may have different professional cultures, priorities, and communication styles that can generate misunderstandings or friction if not skillfully navigated.

Promoting a culture of accountability is another vital aspect of team management. Project managers need to establish transparent performance expectations, timelines, and quality standards, ensuring that every team member understands their roles and responsibilities. This clarity helps maintain focus and drive progress amidst the inevitable challenges of complex IT projects.

Mentorship forms an equally important pillar of leadership. Given the Caribbean's ongoing efforts to cultivate local ICT talent, many organizations face a shortage of highly skilled specialists who can sustain digital transformation over the long term. IT project managers often take on the role of mentors, providing guidance, knowledge transfer, and skills development to junior staff and emerging professionals. This capacity-building focus not only enhances team performance in the short term but also contributes to strengthening the regional ICT workforce, reducing reliance on costly external consultants, and fostering sustainable digital ecosystems.

To effectively manage remote or geographically dispersed teams, project managers increasingly leverage digital collaboration and communication tools such as video conferencing, instant messaging, shared document platforms, and project management software. These tools facilitate real-time coordination, knowledge sharing, and transparency, helping bridge physical distances and enabling cohesive team dynamics.

Furthermore, successful project managers remain attentive to team members' wellbeing and professional development needs, promoting continuous learning and creating opportunities for skill enhancement through workshops, certifications, and cross-functional exposure. This proactive approach supports employee engagement, reduces turnover, and builds a resilient human capital base essential for the Caribbean's digital ambition.

In conclusion, managing multidisciplinary teams in the Caribbean's unique ICT project environment demands a blend of strong leadership, empathetic communication, conflict resolution, and a sustained commitment to mentorship and capacity-building. By nurturing empowered, skilled, and accountable teams, IT project managers lay the groundwork for delivering high-quality ICT solutions that contribute to the region's digital transformation goals.

5. Navigating Organizational Structures

A critical challenge for IT project managers in the Caribbean—especially within the public sector—is effectively navigating the often hierarchical and bureaucratic organizational structures that characterize many government institutions and large organizations.

These complex institutional environments can slow decision-making, complicate resource mobilization, and introduce layers of procedural requirements that require careful management to avoid project delays or derailment.

IT project managers must develop a sophisticated understanding of these organizational dynamics to operate effectively. This entails recognizing formal lines of authority, understanding the roles of key departments and committees, and appreciating the informal networks and power relations that influence decision-making processes. Navigating these structures requires patience, diplomacy, and strategic acumen to work within existing protocols while driving project objectives forward.

Roberts (2020) emphasizes that success in this area hinges on proactive relationship-building with key organizational influencers and decision-makers. These individuals often hold the formal or informal authority to approve project plans, allocate funding, and champion ICT initiatives within their spheres of influence. Building trustful, respectful, and collaborative relationships with such stakeholders enables project managers to elicit the necessary support and resources, resolve bottlenecks, and align ICT priorities with broader institutional mandates.

Acting as intermediaries and advocates, IT project managers must effectively communicate the value and strategic importance of ICT projects in a manner that resonates with institutional goals and political realities. This involves tailoring messages to different audiences, balancing technical rationales with organizational benefits, and remaining sensitive to political dynamics and potential resistance arising from competing interests or changes in leadership.

Moreover, project managers need to be adept at navigating public sector procurement rules, reporting requirements, and budgeting cycles—each of which can introduce procedural complexities. They must also be prepared to work within multi-layered accountability frameworks and comply with regulations related to transparency, audit, and oversight.

Understanding and respecting institutional protocols does not mean passively accepting bureaucratic inertia. Skilled IT project managers leverage their knowledge of organizational culture and politics to identify opportunities for influencing change, streamlining processes, and fostering a culture receptive to innovation. Such strategic navigation enhances project adaptability and resilience within complex environments.

In summary, the ability to maneuver through hierarchical and bureaucratic structures is a defining competency for IT project managers in the Caribbean. By cultivating strong relationships, exercising political and organizational savvy, and acting as effective advocates and facilitators, they can bridge gaps between technology initiatives and institutional realities, thereby unlocking critical resources and support that drive successful ICT project implementation.

6. Cultural Competency and Adaptability

Cultural awareness is an indispensable competency for IT project managers operating within the Caribbean's richly diverse social and organizational landscapes. The region is characterized by a mosaic of cultures, languages, traditions, and historical backgrounds, all of which shape distinct attitudes toward authority, communication styles, interpersonal relationships, and work ethics. For project managers, understanding and navigating this cultural diversity is essential to building trust, fostering collaboration, and effectively leading multidisciplinary teams and stakeholder groups.

In practice, cultural awareness demands that IT project managers attentively observe and interpret local norms and customs, adapting their leadership and communication approaches accordingly. For example, hierarchical respect and deference to seniority may be deeply ingrained in some Caribbean organizations, requiring managers to exhibit appropriate formalities when engaging with leaders or decision-makers. Alternatively, more informal and communal interaction styles prevalent in certain communities might call for an empathetic, participatory leadership approach that emphasizes relationship-building and inclusivity.

Adjusting communication styles is particularly critical. Caribbean societies may differ in their preferred modes of negotiation, conflict resolution, and decision-making— some favoring direct, explicit discourse while others valuing indirect, nuanced interactions. IT project managers must be sensitive to these preferences to avoid misunderstandings, build rapport, and ensure messages related to project goals and expectations are clearly and respectfully conveyed.

Equally important is adaptability—the capacity to respond flexibly and creatively to unforeseen circumstances and challenges that inevitably arise during ICT project implementation in dynamic environments. Caribbean IT projects often encounter unexpected obstacles such as changes in political leadership, resource shortfalls, infrastructure disruptions, or shifting stakeholder priorities. Effective project managers demonstrate an ability to pivot strategies, modify project plans, and explore alternative solutions without compromising overarching project objectives or quality standards.

This adaptability is not merely reactive but proactive; it entails continuous monitoring of the project environment, learning from emerging insights, and fostering a mindset of resilience within teams. Project managers who cultivate adaptive leadership create an organizational culture that embraces change, experimentation, and iterative improvement—qualities essential for navigating the complexities of digital transformation in the Caribbean.

In summary, cultural awareness and adaptability form the dual pillars that underpin effective IT project management in the Caribbean context. By respectfully aligning leadership and communication styles with local cultural norms and maintaining the flexibility to adjust to evolving realities, IT project managers can enhance stakeholder engagement, mitigate conflict, and sustain project momentum. These competencies significantly increase the likelihood of successful ICT project outcomes that are culturally congruent, contextually relevant, and operationally resilient.

7. Problem-Solving and Innovation

Infrastructural limitations and economic constraints are defining features of the Caribbean's development landscape, placing significant demands on IT project managers to exhibit innovative problem-solving capabilities. Effective management in this context often involves developing creative, resource-efficient solutions that enable projects to progress despite restricted budgets, limited access to advanced hardware, and uneven technological infrastructure.

For example, to address frequent shortages of physical IT assets such as servers and networking equipment, project managers increasingly turn to cloud computing services. Cloud platforms offer scalable, flexible, and pay-as-you-go solutions that reduce upfront capital expenditure, lower maintenance burdens, and facilitate remote access to computing resources—thereby overcoming traditional hardware constraints prevalent in many Caribbean organizations.

Similarly, the adoption of open-source software represents another strategic innovation to curtail costs while maintaining functional and customizable ICT solutions. Open-source platforms provide access to robust software tools without expensive licensing fees and offer opportunities to tailor applications to local needs with the support of the global open-source community. Leveraging such technologies allows project teams to redirect scarce financial resources toward other critical project components such as training, connectivity enhancements, or change management.

Roberts (2020) underscores the importance of fostering a culture of innovation within project teams as a critical enabler of effective problem-solving. Encouraging team members to proactively identify both risks and opportunities creates an environment where challenges are anticipated early, and creative solutions can be collaboratively developed. This culture promotes agility and responsiveness, allowing projects to adapt dynamically to evolving conditions, unexpected obstacles, or emerging technologies.

Innovation-driven teams are typically characterized by openness to experimentation, cross-disciplinary collaboration, and a willingness to challenge conventional approaches. Within the Caribbean context, where resource limitations are common and external support can be unpredictable, cultivating such a mindset is essential for enhancing project resilience and ensuring successful outcomes.

Moreover, innovative problem-solving extends beyond technological choices to include process improvements, stakeholder engagement strategies, and risk management techniques that are tailored to local realities. For instance, creative scheduling may mitigate infrastructural downtime, partnerships with local communities can enhance digital literacy efforts, and leveraging mobile-first solutions may increase accessibility in areas with limited fixed-line internet.

In conclusion, innovative problem-solving is both a necessity and a strategic advantage for IT project managers operating in the Caribbean's constrained economic and infrastructural environment. By embracing resourcefulness, harnessing emerging technologies like cloud and open-source platforms, and fostering an innovative culture within their teams, project managers can effectively navigate challenges while unlocking new pathways for digital transformation that are sustainable, scalable, and contextually appropriate.

Navigating Organizational and Cultural Dynamics

The interplay between organizational structures and cultural dynamics constitutes a defining and complex feature of IT project management in the Caribbean. Success in this environment requires project managers to possess not only technical and managerial expertise but also a nuanced understanding of how institutional hierarchies, bureaucratic processes, and deeply rooted cultural norms interact and influence the trajectory and outcomes of ICT initiatives.

Roberts' study offers rich and detailed insights into the multifaceted ways in which these organizational and cultural factors impact project success. For example, hierarchical and often rigid bureaucratic structures within government agencies can slow decision-making, inhibit agile responses to emerging challenges, and create multiple layers of approval that IT project managers must skillfully navigate. Understanding formal authority channels and power dynamics is therefore crucial for securing timely endorsements, resource allocations, and operational support.

Equally important are the informal social networks, relationships, and shared values that permeate organizations and communities in the Caribbean. Cultural attributes—such as respect for seniority, communication styles that may lean toward indirect or high-context interactions, and community-oriented work ethics—shape how stakeholders engage with projects and each other. Misalignment between a project manager's approach and these cultural expectations can lead to misunderstandings, resistance to change, or reduced collaboration.

Roberts emphasizes that effective Caribbean IT project managers deliberately integrate organizational knowledge with cultural sensitivity to build trust, foster cooperation, and facilitate effective communication. This includes adapting leadership styles to local norms, showing respect for institutional protocols, and engaging stakeholders in ways that resonate with their values and expectations. By doing so, they create a conducive environment for shared ownership and collective problem-solving.

The convergence of organizational and cultural dynamics also means that IT project managers must be astute political navigators—balancing competing interests, managing potential conflicts, and leveraging cultural strengths such as communal solidarity and relational networks to enhance project buy-in and sustainability.

Incorporating these insights, project managers in the Caribbean are better positioned to design and implement culturally informed change management strategies, tailor stakeholder engagement approaches, and develop governance frameworks that reflect local realities. This holistic approach strengthens their ability to deliver projects that are not only technically sound but also institutionally embedded and socially accepted.

Organizational Dynamics

Caribbean organizations, particularly within the public sector, often operate within rigid hierarchical structures and highly formalized procedural frameworks. These organizational characteristics, while intended to ensure order and accountability, can inadvertently impede the agility and speed necessary for successful IT project implementation. IT project managers frequently encounter significant delays during critical phases such as obtaining approvals, navigating procurement processes, and securing timely disbursement of funds—all of which can cumulatively slow project progress and challenge tight delivery timelines.

Navigating these structural constraints requires IT project managers to develop well-considered strategies that emphasize collaboration, diplomacy, and adherence to established protocols. Successful managers cultivate productive working relationships with bureaucrats, middle managers, and political leaders alike, recognizing the nuanced importance of timing, formal processes, and institutional etiquette in decision-making. By demonstrating respect for institutional norms and engaging stakeholders through appropriate channels, project managers can build trust, gain legitimacy, and facilitate smoother project advancement even within bureaucratic constraints.

Change management constitutes another critical tool in addressing organizational dynamics. Many staff members within Caribbean organizations may demonstrate resistance to ICT initiatives due to concerns about disruptions to established workflows, fears of job displacement, or unfamiliarity with new technologies. Effective IT project managers employ targeted change management techniques—such as inclusive communication, capacity-building workshops, and participatory feedback mechanisms—to reduce apprehension, build digital literacy, and foster a culture that values innovation and continuous improvement.

Additionally, organizational politics inevitably influence project priorities, resource allocation, and support levels. Competing interests among different departments, power blocs, or external stakeholders can create challenges for aligning ICT projects with wide-ranging institutional goals.

Political considerations may also lead to shifts in project direction or funding interruptions, especially in volatile governance environments. As such, IT project managers must possess a high degree of political savvy—anticipating potential conflicts, understanding stakeholder motivations, and navigating competing agendas to maintain alignment and secure essential backing.

Political astuteness extends to recognizing opportunities where ICT projects can advance visible government or organizational objectives, thereby garnering broader political support. By framing digital initiatives within the context of national development plans or key policy priorities, project managers can enhance project visibility and sustainability.

In summary, the organizational dynamics of Caribbean public sector institutions present complex challenges that require IT project managers to blend technical proficiency with interpersonal acumen and political intelligence. Mastery in working within hierarchical frameworks, negotiating bureaucratic processes, managing resistance to change, and navigating institutional politics is essential to securing the resources, approvals, and support that enable successful ICT project execution. Developing these competencies empowers project managers to turn organizational constraints into manageable factors that, when skillfully navigated, contribute to the overall success and impact of digital transformation efforts in the region.

Cultural Dynamics

Cultural factors exert a profound influence on the way communication, leadership, and teamwork unfold within ICT projects across the Caribbean. One salient cultural trait in many Caribbean societies is a deep respect for seniority, authority, and established hierarchies. While this respect fosters social cohesion and order, it can also inadvertently inhibit open feedback, creative challenge, and critical dialogue—elements that are essential for innovation and problem-solving in technology projects. As a result, IT project managers must deliberately cultivate safe, inclusive spaces where team members feel empowered to share ideas, raise concerns, and engage in constructive debate without fear of reprisal or social discomfort.

Language diversity further complicates communication strategies in the region. Caribbean nations often contain a rich tapestry of languages, dialects, and vernaculars, alongside wide variations in digital and ICT literacy levels among stakeholders and end-users. These differences necessitate tailored, culturally sensitive communication approaches to ensure messages are accessible, relatable, and clearly understood across diverse audiences. For example, using local stories, culturally relevant metaphors, and familiar analogies—rather than purely technical jargon or foreign examples—can significantly enhance comprehension and acceptance of ICT initiatives, thereby fostering greater user engagement and participation.

Additionally, effective community engagement is frequently critical for the success of ICT projects that impact public services such as healthcare, education, and utilities. Given the communal nature and strong social networks characteristic of many Caribbean communities, participatory approaches that actively involve users and local leaders throughout the project lifecycle help build vital trust and social license to operate. Involving communities in needs assessments, design consultations, pilot testing, and feedback sessions ensures that digital solutions are realistic, user-friendly, and aligned with actual needs rather than imposed from external perspectives.

Such participatory engagement not only bridges cultural and social gaps but also promotes transparency, accountability, and ownership of ICT initiatives at grassroots levels. It encourages community members to become champions of technology adoption and advocates for sustained use beyond project completion. This approach also aids in identifying potential social or cultural barriers to digital uptake early on, allowing project managers to adapt strategies accordingly.

Moreover, IT project managers must stay attuned to subtler cultural dynamics—such as attitudes toward risk, collective versus individual decision-making preferences, and the influence of religious or traditional beliefs—that shape stakeholder behavior and acceptance of technological change. Sensitivity to these nuances enables the development of more culturally congruent and respectful project interventions that resonate deeply with the communities served.

In summary, cultural dynamics in the Caribbean significantly shape the communication, leadership, and participatory processes central to IT project success. By fostering open dialogue, customizing communication strategies, and embedding participatory community engagement practices, project managers can navigate cultural complexities effectively. This cultural competence helps to bridge divides, nurture innovation, and ensure that ICT solutions are not only technically sound but socially accepted and sustainably integrated into local contexts.

Balancing Tradition and Innovation

IT project managers operating in the Caribbean face the delicate task of balancing respect for deeply rooted traditional work practices with the imperative to introduce modern information and communication technology (ICT) solutions that drive innovation and efficiency. This balance demands a high degree of diplomacy, cultural intelligence, and emotional sensitivity, as any abrupt or insensitive imposition of new technologies can generate resistance, misunderstandings, or even outright rejection from employees and stakeholders accustomed to longstanding routines and organizational cultures.

Effectively managing this dynamic requires project managers to engage in thoughtful dialogue, listening attentively to concerns anchored in tradition while clearly communicating the benefits and relevance of ICT innovations. They must ensure that the introduction of new systems is framed not as a threat to existing practices but as an enhancement that supports and strengthens established workflows. By validating the importance of traditional methods and showing respect for institutional heritage, project managers can create a more receptive environment where technology adoption is viewed as complementary rather than disruptive.

Roberts (2020) identifies collaborative leadership as a particularly effective approach in this setting. Collaborative leaders emphasize inclusiveness and participation, actively involving diverse stakeholders—including frontline staff, managers, and community representatives—in decision-making processes. Through fostering a culture of mutual respect, these leaders encourage open dialogue that acknowledges and integrates differing perspectives, thereby reducing resistance and building broad-based consensus around shared project goals.

Such leadership practices support the co-creation of solutions—where project teams collectively adapt ICT initiatives to fit local contexts and address user needs—enhancing both relevance and ownership. Collaborative leadership also facilitates knowledge sharing and capacity building, enabling team members to evolve alongside technological changes rather than feeling sidelined.

In addition, this leadership style nurtures trust between project managers and stakeholders, which is vital in contexts where skepticism of external expertise or new approaches may be prevalent. When staff and communities feel heard, valued, and meaningfully engaged, they are more likely to embrace innovation with confidence and commitment.

In summary, successfully introducing modern ICT solutions within the Caribbean's rich tapestry of traditional practices requires IT project managers to exhibit exceptional cultural intelligence and diplomatic agility. By adopting a collaborative leadership approach—characterized by participation, respect for diversity, and consensus-building—they can navigate potential conflicts, reconcile tradition with innovation, and foster an inclusive environment conducive to sustainable digital transformation.

Conclusion

The role of IT project managers in the Caribbean is inherently multifaceted, complex, and absolutely vital to the region's ongoing digital advancement. Far beyond serving as mere technical experts, these professionals assume critical roles as strategic leaders, effective communicators, and skilled cultural navigators, all of which are essential for bridging the gap between sophisticated ICT innovations and the diverse, resource-constrained realities of Caribbean institutions.

Their ability to manage and operate within complex organizational structures—characterized by hierarchical public sector institutions and dynamic private sector environments—combined with their sensitivity to deep-seated cultural nuances, is key to ensuring the successful integration and adoption of digital technologies. Navigating these organizational and cultural landscapes requires not only formal project management skills but also emotional intelligence, political acumen, and a collaborative leadership style that embraces inclusivity and fosters stakeholder ownership.

A broad and diversified skill set is therefore indispensable for Caribbean IT project managers. In addition to technical proficiency in project methodologies, ICT architectures, and problem-solving strategies, they must excel in strategic planning, effectively engage and communicate with multi-sector stakeholders, demonstrate strong leadership capabilities, and exhibit high cultural competency. This comprehensive capacity equips project managers to overcome the unique challenges posed by infrastructural limitations, bureaucratic inertia, resistance to change, and economic constraints that are prevalent across the region.

The work of these project managers directly supports national and regional ambitions to create sustainable digital economies that empower citizens, improve governance, enhance public service delivery, and ultimately foster better socio-economic conditions. Their role aligns closely with broader developmental objectives, including those outlined in national ICT policies, regional integration frameworks, and international goals such as the United Nations Sustainable Development Goals (SDGs).

Roberts' doctoral study underscores the pressing need for the development and adoption of tailored IT project management frameworks that are contextually relevant to Caribbean realities. These specialized frameworks should integrate global best practices with local cultural, organizational, and economic considerations, providing adaptive tools and methodologies that enhance project success rates. Furthermore, Roberts advocates for sustained and targeted professional development programs designed to continuously build the capabilities of IT project managers, keeping pace with rapidly evolving technologies, emerging digital risks, and shifting stakeholder expectations.

By strategically investing in the capacity-building of IT project managers—through certification programs, mentoring, peer learning networks, and institutional support—the Caribbean region can markedly accelerate its digital transformation journey. Strengthening these professionals' competencies and empowering them to lead effectively will be instrumental in realizing a future where the Caribbean emerges as a digitally inclusive, competitive, and resilient region that harnesses ICT as a driver of economic growth and social progress.

Chapter 3

Strategies for Successful ICT Integration

Overview of Effective Strategies Identified in Research

The integration of Information and Communication Technologies (ICTs) within organizations in the Eastern Caribbean presents unique challenges and opportunities. Drawing from Carl S. Roberts' doctoral study (2020), this chapter outlines the effective strategies employed by IT project managers to successfully implement ICT projects in this context. The research, grounded in the Technology Acceptance Model (TAM), highlights that successful ICT integration hinges on a combination of technical, managerial, and socio-cultural strategies tailored to the Caribbean environment.

One of the foremost strategies identified is **the management of organizational structure**. Roberts (2020) found that IT project managers who proactively engage with and adapt to the hierarchical and bureaucratic nature of Caribbean institutions are better positioned to secure project buy-in and resources. This involves building strong relationships with key stakeholders across government and private sectors, understanding decision-making processes, and aligning project goals with organizational priorities. By navigating these structures adeptly, project managers facilitate smoother approval processes and foster a culture receptive to ICT adoption.

Another critical strategy is the **implementation of government-wide area networks (WANs)** designed to enable ICT-enabled services across business, education, and government sectors. This infrastructure backbone is essential for fostering innovation and digital transformation. IT project managers focus on ensuring that such networks are scalable, secure, and accessible, thereby creating a platform for e-government services, e-commerce, and online learning. The study emphasizes that successful WAN deployment requires meticulous planning, stakeholder cooperation, and ongoing maintenance strategies that consider the region's infrastructural constraints.

Budget management, stakeholder buy-in, and addressing integration challenges form the third major theme. Effective ICT integration requires **transparent budgeting processes** that reflect realistic costs and contingencies. IT project managers employ strategies to secure funding by demonstrating the socio-economic benefits of ICT projects, thus enhancing stakeholder confidence. Moreover, they actively manage resistance by communicating the value of ICT initiatives and involving end-users in the adoption process. Challenges such as limited technical skills, infrastructure gaps, and political changes are mitigated through continuous training, phased implementation, and adaptive project management methodologies.

Roberts (2020) also underscores the importance of **developing IT implementation frameworks aligned with established project management methodologies**, such as the Project Management Body of Knowledge (PMBOK). These frameworks incorporate remedial measures to address common pitfalls in ICT projects, including scope creep, inadequate risk management, and poor communication. By tailoring these frameworks to local realities, IT project managers can better control project variables and deliver outcomes that meet organizational objectives.

In summary, the research identifies a multifaceted approach combining organizational savvy, technical infrastructure development, financial stewardship, and adaptive project management as key to successful ICT integration in the Eastern Caribbean.

Adapting Global Best Practices to Local Realities

While global best practices in ICT project management provide valuable guidance, their direct application in the Caribbean context often requires significant adaptation. Roberts (2020) highlights that the socio-economic, cultural, and infrastructural realities of the Eastern Caribbean necessitate a localized approach to ICT integration.

One core adaptation involves **contextualizing project management methodologies**. Standard frameworks like PMBOK and Agile emphasize structured processes and stakeholder engagement, but Caribbean IT project managers modify these to account for limited resources, fluctuating political support, and varying levels of ICT literacy. For example, phased rollouts and incremental implementation allow projects to progress despite funding uncertainties or infrastructural limitations. This staged approach also provides opportunities for feedback and adjustment, increasing the likelihood of sustained adoption.

Another adaptation concerns **cultural sensitivity and communication styles**. The Caribbean's diverse cultural landscape influences how authority is perceived, how feedback is given, and how collaboration unfolds. IT project managers must employ culturally appropriate communication methods, often relying on face-to-face interactions, storytelling, and community engagement to build trust and encourage participation. Recognizing the importance of relationships and respect for hierarchy helps in overcoming resistance and fostering cooperation.

Capacity building and training are also tailored to local needs. Rather than assuming baseline ICT skills, project managers design training programs that accommodate varying levels of digital literacy. These programs often include hands-on workshops, mentoring, and ongoing support to empower end-users and reduce dependency on external consultants.

Furthermore, **resource constraints** such as limited hardware, unreliable internet connectivity, and budgetary restrictions require innovative solutions. IT project managers in the Caribbean frequently leverage cloud computing, open-source software, and partnerships with regional and international organizations to supplement local capabilities. These strategies help bridge infrastructural gaps and reduce costs while maintaining project viability.

Importantly, **political and institutional dynamics** are factored into project planning. Given the influence of political cycles and bureaucratic processes, IT project managers build flexibility into timelines and develop contingency plans for leadership changes or policy shifts. Engaging political champions and aligning projects with national development agendas enhance project legitimacy and sustainability.

Roberts' study suggests that successful ICT integration in the Caribbean is less about rigid adherence to global best practices and more about **adaptive implementation**— blending proven methodologies with local knowledge, cultural understanding, and pragmatic innovation.

Case Study: A Successful ICT Project in the Eastern Caribbean

To illustrate the application of these strategies, Roberts (2020) presents a detailed case study of a government-wide area network (WAN) implementation project in one Eastern Caribbean country. This project aimed to connect multiple government agencies, educational institutions, and business entities to facilitate e-government services and foster a digital economy.

Project Background:

The initiative was launched to address fragmented ICT infrastructures that hindered communication and service delivery across government departments. The WAN was envisioned as a backbone to support online services, improve data sharing, and enable remote learning and business transactions.

Strategic Planning and Stakeholder Engagement:

From the outset, the IT project manager prioritized stakeholder engagement, conducting workshops and consultations with government officials, educators, and business leaders. This inclusive approach helped identify user requirements, build consensus, and secure political and financial support.

Recognizing the bureaucratic environment, the project manager established clear communication channels and governance structures. A steering committee comprising representatives from key agencies was formed to oversee progress and address challenges collaboratively.

Technical Implementation:

The project adopted a phased deployment strategy, starting with pilot sites in the capital and gradually expanding to rural areas. This approach allowed the team to test technologies, train users, and refine processes before full-scale rollout.

To overcome infrastructural challenges, the project leveraged a hybrid network architecture combining fiber optics in urban centers with wireless links for remote locations. Open-source network management tools were employed to reduce costs and increase flexibility.

Capacity Building:

Comprehensive training programs were integral to the project. End-users received hands-on workshops tailored to their roles, while technical staff underwent advanced training to manage and maintain the network. Ongoing support and knowledge-sharing forums fostered a community of practice that sustained the network's operation.

Budget and Risk Management:

The project manager developed a detailed budget with contingencies for unexpected costs. Regular financial reviews and transparent reporting ensured accountability and maintained stakeholder confidence.

Risk management plans addressed potential obstacles such as equipment delays, political changes, and resistance from staff. Mitigation strategies included alternative suppliers, advocacy with political leaders, and change management initiatives to ease transitions.

Outcomes and Impact:

The WAN project successfully connected over 50 government offices and educational institutions within two years. It enabled the launch of e-government portals, improved data sharing, and supported remote education during crises.

The project also stimulated business innovation by providing reliable internet access and fostering e-commerce opportunities. Importantly, it demonstrated that tailored strategies combining technical excellence, stakeholder engagement, and cultural adaptation can overcome the Caribbean's unique challenges.

Conclusion

Successful ICT integration in the Eastern Caribbean requires a holistic approach that blends global best practices with local realities. Roberts' doctoral research identifies key strategies—managing organizational structures, building robust technical infrastructures, securing stakeholder buy-in, and adapting methodologies—that empower IT project managers to navigate the region's complex socio-economic and cultural landscape.

The case study of the government-wide area network exemplifies how these strategies translate into tangible outcomes that advance digital transformation and socio-economic development. By fostering inclusive planning, phased implementation, capacity building, and adaptive risk management, Caribbean ICT projects can achieve sustainable success.

This chapter underscores the importance of context-sensitive approaches and continuous learning for IT project managers committed to driving positive change through ICT integration in the Caribbean and similar developing regions.

Chapter 4

Organizational Management and Leadership

Building Supportive Organizational Cultures

Organizational culture is much more than a set of written policies or slogans; it is the living, breathing essence of how an organization operates and evolves. It influences every aspect of work life, from decision-making and innovation to employee satisfaction and retention. In the context of ICT adoption, culture becomes a critical determinant of success or failure. When organizations foster a culture that is supportive, adaptive, and forward-looking, they create a fertile environment for technological innovation to thrive.

A supportive organizational culture is rooted in shared values that prioritize learning, collaboration, and openness. This means encouraging employees to voice ideas without fear of judgment, to experiment with new tools, and to view mistakes as learning opportunities rather than failures. Such a culture reduces the fear and uncertainty that often accompany technological change, replacing it with curiosity and enthusiasm.

Leaders have a pivotal role in shaping this culture. Their behavior sets the tone for the entire organization. For example, when leaders openly embrace new technologies and demonstrate a willingness to learn alongside their teams, they signal that change is not only necessary but also desirable. This modeling behavior encourages employees to follow suit. Conversely, if leaders resist change or fail to communicate its importance, employees are likely to mirror that resistance, creating a culture of stagnation.

Building this culture requires deliberate effort. Organizations should invest in initiatives that promote inclusivity and diversity, recognizing that a variety of perspectives enrich problem-solving and innovation. For instance, cross-functional teams that bring together IT specialists, end-users, and business leaders can foster mutual understanding and more effective technology solutions. Additionally, continuous learning should be embedded into the organizational fabric through regular training sessions, workshops, and informal knowledge exchanges. This ongoing development helps employees stay current with technological trends and reduces anxiety about obsolescence.

Recognition programs that reward innovation, collaboration, and adaptability further reinforce cultural values. Celebrating small wins related to ICT adoption— such as successful pilot projects or creative uses of new software—builds momentum and motivates others to engage. Psychological safety, a concept championed by organizational psychologists, is particularly crucial. When employees trust that their ideas and concerns will be heard without reprisal, they are more likely to take the risks necessary for innovation.

Finally, culture must be aligned with the organization's strategic vision. If the overarching goal is to become a digitally agile enterprise, then values like agility, customer focus, and innovation must permeate every level of the organization. This alignment ensures that ICT adoption is not seen as a one-off project but as a fundamental shift in how the organization operates and delivers value.

The Role of Organizational Structure and Leadership

The research conducted in the Eastern Caribbean underscores the profound influence of organizational structure on ICT integration. A rigid, hierarchical structure can stifle innovation and slow down decision-making processes, while a more flexible, decentralized approach empowers teams to act swiftly and creatively. IT project managers interviewed in the study consistently highlighted the need for structures that facilitate open communication and cross-functional collaboration.

Leaders, therefore, must not only champion ICT initiatives but also be architects of structures that dismantle silos and encourage knowledge sharing. In practice, this often means establishing steering committees or task forces that include representatives from all stakeholder groups—IT, business units, end-users, and even external partners. These bodies serve as forums for dialogue, feedback, and consensus-building, ensuring that ICT projects are not imposed from the top down but co-created with those who will use and sustain them.

Moreover, the leadership's commitment to continuous improvement is vital. As the study revealed, organizations that regularly assess and refine their processes—through mechanisms such as after-action reviews, feedback loops, and performance metrics—are better positioned to adapt to the evolving demands of digital transformation. Leaders who model a growth mindset, openly acknowledge setbacks, and celebrate learning foster resilience and adaptability throughout the organization.

Fostering Buy-In and Reducing Resistance

One of the most significant challenges identified in the thesis is achieving buy-in from all levels of the organization. Resistance to change is a natural human response, particularly when it involves unfamiliar technologies or threatens established routines. The Technology Acceptance Model (TAM), which underpins much of the research, emphasizes the importance of perceived usefulness and perceived ease of use in driving acceptance. However, these perceptions are themselves shaped by organizational culture.

To build a culture that supports buy-in, organizations must engage in transparent, two-way communication. This involves not only articulating the strategic rationale for ICT adoption but also listening to the concerns and aspirations of employees. Town hall meetings, focus groups, and anonymous surveys can provide valuable insights into the sources of resistance and the levers of motivation.

The research in the Eastern Caribbean found that involving employees early and often in the design and implementation of ICT initiatives leads to greater ownership and enthusiasm. When staff see their input reflected in the final solution—whether it's a new software platform or a reengineered business process—they are more likely to champion the change among their peers.

Additionally, organizations should address practical barriers to adoption, such as inadequate training, insufficient resources, or unclear expectations. Providing comprehensive onboarding programs, user-friendly documentation, and responsive support services can alleviate anxiety and build confidence. Recognition and reward systems that acknowledge early adopters and innovators further reinforce the desired behaviors and attitudes.

The Importance of Inclusivity and Diversity

A recurring theme in the study is the value of inclusivity and diversity in driving successful ICT integration. Diverse teams bring a wider range of experiences, perspectives, and problem-solving approaches, which can lead to more creative and effective solutions. In the context of the Eastern Caribbean, this means not only bridging generational and functional divides within organizations but also respecting and leveraging cultural differences across the region.

Inclusive cultures are characterized by psychological safety, where all voices are heard and valued. This is particularly important in environments where hierarchical norms may discourage junior staff or minority groups from speaking up. Leaders must actively solicit input from all quarters, create safe spaces for dissent, and ensure that decision-making processes are transparent and equitable.

The study's participants noted that cross-functional teams—comprising IT professionals, business leaders, and end-users—were instrumental in surfacing hidden challenges and uncovering innovative opportunities during ICT projects. These teams were most effective when they operated in environments that valued diversity of thought and fostered mutual respect.

Embedding Continuous Learning and Development

The pace of technological change demands that organizations become learning organizations—entities that continuously acquire, share, and apply new knowledge. The thesis highlights the importance of ongoing professional development in building a culture that is resilient to disruption and open to innovation.

Continuous learning can take many forms, from formal training programs and certifications to informal mentoring and peer-to-peer knowledge exchanges. Organizations should create opportunities for employees to experiment with new tools, attend industry conferences, and participate in online learning communities. Importantly, learning should be recognized and rewarded, not just in terms of individual achievement but as a collective endeavor that advances the organization's mission.

The research also points to the value of learning from failure. When mistakes are treated as opportunities for growth rather than grounds for punishment, employees are more willing to take calculated risks and push the boundaries of what is possible. This mindset is essential for fostering innovation and maintaining a competitive edge in the digital economy.

Recognition, Motivation, and Psychological Safety

Recognition is a powerful lever for shaping organizational culture. The study found that organizations that celebrated small wins—such as the successful rollout of a new application or the creative use of existing technologies— were more likely to sustain momentum and keep teams engaged. Recognition need not always be monetary; public acknowledgment, opportunities for career advancement, and visible leadership support can be equally motivating.

Psychological safety, as championed by organizational psychologists, emerged as a critical enabler of innovation. When employees trust that their ideas and concerns will be heard without fear of reprisal, they are more likely to experiment, collaborate, and contribute to the organization's digital transformation journey. Leaders play a central role in modeling vulnerability, admitting their own uncertainties, and encouraging open dialogue.

Aligning Culture with Strategic Vision

Perhaps the most important insight from the research is the need to align organizational culture with strategic objectives. In the Eastern Caribbean context, many organizations articulated ambitious visions of digital transformation and economic modernization. However, these aspirations could only be realized when cultural values—such as agility, customer focus, and innovation—were deeply embedded at every level.

This alignment requires more than rhetoric; it demands deliberate action. Organizations must ensure that their recruitment, onboarding, performance management, and succession planning processes all reinforce the desired culture. Strategic initiatives—such as the creation of government-wide area networks or the promotion of e-services—must be supported by cultural norms that embrace change, value learning, and reward collaboration.

The study's participants emphasized the importance of leadership in driving this alignment. Leaders must be visible champions of the digital agenda, consistently communicating its importance and demonstrating its relevance through their own actions. They must also be willing to challenge entrenched norms and practices that are inconsistent with the organization's strategic direction.

Overcoming Regional Challenges: Lessons from the Eastern Caribbean

The unique context of the Eastern Caribbean presents both challenges and opportunities for building supportive organizational cultures. Limited resources, infrastructural constraints, and historical legacies of centralized decision-making can impede progress. However, the region's close-knit communities, strong traditions of collaboration, and shared aspirations for socio-economic development provide fertile ground for cultural transformation.

The research identified several strategies that were particularly effective in the Caribbean context:

1. **Leveraging Regional Networks**: Organizations that participated in regional forums and knowledge-sharing initiatives were better able to access best practices, avoid common pitfalls, and build collective capacity for ICT integration.
2. **Tailoring Solutions to Local Realities**: Successful ICT projects were those that respected local customs, languages, and business practices. This required a deep understanding of the social and cultural context, as well as a willingness to adapt global solutions to local needs.
3. **Building Public-Private Partnerships**: Collaboration between government, industry, and civil society was critical for overcoming resource constraints and achieving scale. These partnerships

enabled organizations to pool expertise, share risks, and align incentives.

4. **Promoting Digital Literacy**: Widespread digital literacy initiatives—targeting not just employees but also the broader community—helped to demystify technology and build a culture of curiosity and experimentation.

5. **Encouraging Grassroots Innovation**: Some of the most impactful ICT solutions emerged from the grassroots, where frontline employees identified and addressed pressing challenges. Organizations that empowered these innovators and provided platforms for scaling their ideas reaped significant benefits.

Sustaining Cultural Change: A Long-Term Commitment

Building a supportive organizational culture is not a one-time effort but an ongoing journey. The research underscores the importance of sustained leadership commitment, regular assessment, and continuous improvement. Organizations must be vigilant against complacency, recognizing that culture can drift over time and that new challenges will inevitably arise.

To sustain momentum, organizations should:

- Regularly assess cultural health through surveys, focus groups, and performance metrics.

- Celebrate progress and acknowledge setbacks, using both as opportunities for learning and growth.
- Invest in leadership development to ensure that future leaders are equipped to champion the desired culture.
- Maintain open channels of communication to surface emerging issues and opportunities.
- Adapt policies and practices to reflect changing realities and evolving strategic priorities.

A supportive organizational culture is the bedrock upon which successful ICT adoption and digital transformation are built. It enables organizations to navigate the complexities of technological change, harness the creativity and commitment of their people, and deliver lasting value to stakeholders.

The lessons from the Eastern Caribbean are clear: culture matters. By investing in inclusive, adaptive, and forward-looking cultures, organizations can unlock the full potential of ICT and drive sustainable development in the digital age.

Change Management Strategies for ICT Adoption

The process of adopting Information and Communication Technologies (ICT) is inherently disruptive. It challenges established workflows, redefines roles, and requires new skills. Without effective change management, these disruptions can lead to resistance, low morale, and wasted investments. Change management is therefore not optional but essential for ensuring that technology initiatives achieve their intended outcomes.

A successful change management strategy begins with a comprehensive understanding of the current organizational landscape. This includes assessing technological readiness, employee attitudes, and existing processes. For example, conducting surveys or focus groups can reveal concerns or misconceptions about the new technology. Identifying these early allows leaders to tailor communication and training efforts to address specific issues.

The planning phase translates this understanding into a detailed roadmap. This roadmap outlines key milestones, responsible parties, resource allocation, and communication plans. It also identifies quick wins—early successes that demonstrate the benefits of change and build confidence. For instance, implementing a user-friendly feature that immediately improves daily tasks can generate positive buzz and reduce skepticism.

During the transformation phase, the focus shifts to execution and support. Training programs should be customized to different user groups, recognizing that a one-size-fits-all approach is ineffective. Hands-on workshops, online tutorials, and peer mentoring can cater to diverse learning styles. Coaching and mentoring provide personalized support, helping employees overcome specific challenges and build competence.

Leaders must also maintain visible engagement throughout this phase. Their active participation in training sessions, open forums, and feedback mechanisms signals commitment and helps sustain momentum. Communication should be frequent, transparent, and two-way, allowing employees to express concerns and receive timely responses.

The final stage—feedback and adjustment—is critical for sustaining change. Organizations should establish metrics to track adoption rates, user satisfaction, and performance improvements. Regular feedback loops enable continuous refinement of strategies. For example, if a particular department struggles with a new system, targeted interventions can be deployed. This iterative process fosters a culture of continuous improvement and ensures that ICT adoption is not a one-time event but an ongoing evolution.

Overall, change management must address both the technical and human sides of ICT adoption. Technology alone cannot transform an organization; it is the people who use it that ultimately determine success. By focusing on human factors, organizations can convert resistance into enthusiasm and embed new ways of working into their DNA.

Integrating Change Management with the Technology Acceptance Model (TAM)

A central insight from the thesis is the value of aligning change management strategies with established theoretical frameworks, particularly the Technology Acceptance Model (TAM). TAM posits that two key factors— perceived usefulness and perceived ease of use—drive user acceptance of new technologies. Change management initiatives should therefore be designed to enhance these perceptions among all stakeholders.

Assessing Readiness and Building Awareness

The first step in any change management process is to assess organizational readiness. This involves evaluating the current state of ICT infrastructure, the digital literacy of staff, and the prevailing attitudes toward technology. In the Eastern Caribbean context, the research found that readiness assessments were often overlooked, leading to mismatches between technological solutions and organizational needs.

To address this, project managers should conduct comprehensive readiness assessments using surveys, interviews, and document reviews. These assessments should not only gauge technical capacity but also surface cultural and psychological barriers to change. For example, some employees may fear job displacement or feel overwhelmed by the pace of technological innovation. By identifying these concerns early, leaders can develop targeted interventions to build awareness and reduce anxiety.

Strategic Communication: Clarity, Consistency, and Engagement

Effective communication is the linchpin of successful change management. In the cases studied, organizations that communicated clearly and consistently about the purpose, benefits, and expectations of ICT initiatives experienced higher levels of buy-in and lower resistance. Communication should be multi-directional, allowing for feedback and dialogue rather than simply broadcasting information.

Key strategies include:

- Developing a communication plan that outlines key messages, channels, and timing.
- Utilizing multiple formats—emails, town halls, posters, intranet updates—to reach diverse audiences.
- Highlighting success stories and quick wins to build momentum.
- Addressing rumors and misinformation promptly to maintain trust.

Leaders and change champions should be visible and accessible, modeling openness and responsiveness. In the Eastern Caribbean, leveraging respected figures within the organization—such as department heads or long-serving employees—as change ambassadors proved particularly effective.

Training and Capacity Building: Tailoring to Diverse Needs

The thesis emphasizes that training is not a one-off event but a continuous process. Effective change management recognizes the diversity of learning styles and technical competencies within the workforce. A mix of training modalities—classroom sessions, e-learning modules, hands-on workshops, and peer mentoring—ensures that all employees have access to the support they need.

In the Caribbean context, peer mentoring and informal knowledge sharing were especially valuable. Employees often learned best from colleagues who understood their local context and could provide practical, relevant advice. Organizations should formalize these peer support networks, recognizing and rewarding those who contribute to the learning of others.

Furthermore, training should be role-specific. For example, frontline staff may need basic digital literacy skills, while managers require training in data-driven decision-making and change leadership. Regular refresher courses and updates are essential to keep pace with evolving technologies and business processes.

Leadership and Stakeholder Engagement

Leadership commitment is a recurring theme in the thesis findings. Leaders must not only endorse ICT initiatives but also actively participate in the change process. This includes attending training sessions, soliciting feedback, and addressing concerns directly. Their visible engagement signals the importance of the change and helps to overcome skepticism.

Stakeholder engagement extends beyond internal staff. In the Eastern Caribbean, successful ICT projects often involved external partners—vendors, consultants, government agencies, and even end-users in the broader community. Early and ongoing engagement with these stakeholders ensures alignment of goals and expectations, reduces resistance, and fosters a sense of shared ownership.

Managing Resistance: Understanding and Addressing Concerns

Resistance to change is natural, particularly when it threatens established routines or job security. The thesis identifies several sources of resistance in the Caribbean context, including fear of redundancy, lack of confidence in new systems, and skepticism about management's motives.

Effective change management does not seek to suppress resistance but to understand and address it. This can be achieved through:

- Open forums and listening sessions where employees can voice concerns.
- Anonymous surveys to surface hidden anxieties.
- Targeted support for those most affected by the change, such as retraining or role redefinition.
- Involving resisters in pilot projects or working groups, giving them a stake in the outcome.

By treating resistance as valuable feedback, organizations can adapt their strategies and build greater buy-in.

Monitoring, Evaluation, and Continuous Improvement

Change management is an iterative process. The thesis highlights the importance of establishing clear metrics to monitor progress and impact. These may include:

- Adoption rates (e.g., percentage of staff using new systems)
- User satisfaction scores
- Performance improvements (e.g., reduced processing times, error rates)
- Cost savings or revenue gains

Regular review meetings and feedback loops allow organizations to identify challenges early and make necessary adjustments. In the Caribbean cases studied, organizations that embraced a culture of continuous improvement—celebrating successes, learning from failures, and iterating on their approaches—were more successful in sustaining change.

Case Insights: Change Management in the Eastern Caribbean

Drawing from the empirical findings of the thesis, several practical lessons emerge for ICT change management in the Eastern Caribbean:

1. Management of Organizational Structure

A flexible, responsive organizational structure is critical for successful ICT adoption. Rigid hierarchies can slow decision-making and stifle innovation, while cross-functional teams and decentralized authority enable faster adaptation. Project managers in the study advocated for the creation of steering committees and working groups that included representatives from all affected departments.

2. Government Wide Area Networks and Shared Services

Implementing shared ICT infrastructure—such as government-wide area networks—requires extensive coordination and change management. The thesis documents how phased rollouts, pilot projects, and demonstration sites helped to build confidence and iron out technical issues before full-scale deployment.

3. Budget, Buy-In, and Overcoming Challenges

Resource constraints are a persistent challenge in the region. Change management strategies must therefore be realistic about what can be achieved with available budgets and seek to maximize impact through prioritization and phased implementation. Building buy-in often requires demonstrating tangible benefits early—such as cost savings, improved service delivery, or enhanced user convenience.

4. Cultural Sensitivity and Local Context

ICT change management in the Caribbean must be attuned to local cultures and values. This includes respecting traditional ways of working, recognizing the influence of community leaders, and adapting communication styles to local norms. Successful change leaders in the study were those who built trust, listened actively, and demonstrated cultural competence.

Embedding Change Management into Organizational DNA

For ICT adoption to be sustainable, change management must become part of the organization's ongoing practice, not just a one-off project. This involves:

- Institutionalizing change management roles (e.g., appointing change managers or champions)
- Embedding change management processes into project management methodologies
- Providing ongoing training and professional development
- Recognizing and rewarding adaptability and innovation
- Fostering a culture of learning and continuous improvement

The thesis recommends that organizations in the Caribbean develop formal IT implementation frameworks that integrate change management principles, drawing on best practices from the Project Management Body of Knowledge (PMBOK) and other global standards.

Implications for Social and Economic Development

Effective change management in ICT adoption has far-reaching implications beyond organizational performance. As highlighted in the thesis, successful ICT integration can:

- Lower barriers to starting and growing businesses
- Enable e-commerce and online learning
- Improve public service delivery and transparency
- Empower citizens and communities
- Enhance regional competitiveness in the digital economy

By investing in robust change management strategies, organizations contribute to broader goals of social and economic transformation.

Change management is the bridge between technological innovation and organizational transformation. It is both an art and a science, requiring empathy, strategic thinking, and disciplined execution. The experiences of IT project managers in the Eastern Caribbean demonstrate that while the path to ICT adoption is complex, it is navigable with the right strategies.

By grounding change management in a deep understanding of people, processes, and context—and by leveraging frameworks like TAM—organizations can turn disruption into opportunity. The journey is ongoing, but with commitment and adaptability, ICT adoption can become a catalyst for lasting positive change.

Leadership Lessons from Regional IT Managers

Regional IT managers occupy a unique leadership position that demands both technical expertise and cultural sensitivity. Their experiences navigating ICT adoption across diverse environments yield important lessons for broader organizational leadership. In the context of the Eastern Caribbean, where infrastructural, economic, and cultural conditions vary widely, these lessons are especially instructive for organizations seeking to drive digital transformation and sustainable development.

Visionary Leadership: Charting a Clear Course

One fundamental lesson is the power of visionary leadership. Effective IT managers articulate a clear and compelling vision that links technology to tangible business outcomes. This vision acts as a beacon, guiding teams through uncertainty and complexity. For example, a regional IT manager might frame ICT adoption as a means to improve customer service or streamline operations, making the change relevant and motivating.

The thesis underscores that visionary leaders are those who can translate abstract technological goals into concrete benefits for both staff and stakeholders. By continually communicating the "why" behind ICT initiatives, these leaders foster a sense of purpose and shared direction. In the Eastern Caribbean context, where skepticism about the value of new technology can be high, this clarity of purpose is crucial for building trust and engagement.

Adaptability: Navigating Local Realities

Adaptability is another critical trait. Regional managers often face varying local conditions—differences in infrastructure, workforce skills, and cultural attitudes toward technology. Leaders who foster a culture of learning and flexibility enable their teams to respond creatively to these challenges. They encourage experimentation and view setbacks as opportunities to refine approaches rather than as failures.

The research found that managers who succeeded in integrating ICTs were those who embraced change as a continuous process, not a one-time event. They adapted global best practices to the local context, recognizing that what works in one island or department may not work in another. This flexibility extended to project planning, resource allocation, and even communication styles, allowing managers to pivot quickly in response to emerging challenges or opportunities.

Empathy and Engagement: Leading with Humanity

Empathy and engagement are equally important. Understanding the human side of change allows leaders to design communication and support strategies that resonate with employees. For instance, acknowledging the stress that comes with learning new systems and providing emotional support can ease transitions. Engaged leaders who listen actively and respond to concerns build trust and reduce resistance.

The thesis highlights that successful IT managers in the Caribbean invested significant time in relationship-building. They held open forums, conducted one-on-one check-ins, and created safe spaces for feedback. By demonstrating genuine care for employee well-being, these leaders fostered psychological safety—a key ingredient for innovation and risk-taking. Empathy also extended to understanding the broader social and cultural context, ensuring that ICT initiatives were inclusive and sensitive to local values.

Collaboration: Breaking Down Silos

Collaboration is a hallmark of successful regional IT leadership. Breaking down silos and fostering partnerships across departments and regions enhances resource sharing and innovation. Regional managers who cultivate strong networks can leverage diverse expertise to solve complex problems and accelerate ICT adoption.

The research found that cross-functional teams, comprising IT specialists, business leaders, and end-users, were instrumental in driving successful ICT projects. These teams facilitated mutual learning, surfaced hidden challenges, and generated creative solutions. Managers who encouraged collaboration not only within their organizations but also with external partners—such as government agencies, vendors, and regional bodies—were able to pool resources, share risks, and scale successful initiatives more effectively.

Resilience and Persistence: Sustaining Momentum

Finally, resilience and persistence are indispensable. ICT adoption is rarely smooth; it involves technical glitches, budget constraints, and cultural pushback. Leaders who maintain focus, adapt strategies as needed, and communicate consistently sustain momentum and guide their organizations through challenges.

The thesis documents numerous instances where IT managers faced setbacks—whether due to funding shortfalls, resistance from key stakeholders, or unforeseen technical hurdles. What distinguished the most effective leaders was their ability to persevere, learn from failures, and keep their teams motivated. They celebrated small wins, acknowledged setbacks without assigning blame, and maintained a long-term perspective on digital transformation.

Practical Leadership Strategies from the Field

Drawing from the qualitative interviews and thematic analysis in the thesis, several practical strategies emerge that regional IT managers used to lead successful ICT integration:

1. Aligning Technology with Organizational Goals

Regional IT managers emphasized the importance of ensuring that ICT initiatives are tightly aligned with the organization's strategic objectives. This alignment requires ongoing dialogue with senior leadership, clear documentation of expected outcomes, and regular progress reviews. By framing technology projects as enablers of broader business goals—such as improved service delivery, operational efficiency, or enhanced competitiveness—managers secured executive support and sustained investment.

2. Building Capacity and Empowering Teams

Capacity building was a recurring theme in the research. Managers recognized that successful ICT adoption depended on the skills and confidence of their teams. They invested in continuous training, mentoring, and knowledge-sharing initiatives, often tailoring programs to the specific needs of different user groups. Peer mentoring and informal learning networks were particularly effective in the Caribbean context, where trust and personal relationships are highly valued.

Empowerment also meant giving teams the autonomy to experiment, make decisions, and take ownership of projects. Managers who delegated authority and encouraged initiative fostered a sense of accountability and pride among staff, which translated into higher engagement and better outcomes.

3. Communicating Transparently and Frequently

Transparent and frequent communication was identified as a critical success factor. Managers used a variety of channels—emails, town halls, workshops, and informal gatherings—to keep staff informed and engaged. They were proactive in addressing rumors, clarifying expectations, and providing updates on progress and challenges. Two-way communication was prioritized, with managers actively soliciting feedback and involving employees in decision-making processes.

4. Managing Stakeholder Relationships

The research highlighted the complexity of stakeholder management in regional ICT projects. Successful managers mapped out all relevant stakeholders—internal and external—and developed tailored engagement strategies for each. They built coalitions of support, identified potential resisters early, and worked to address their concerns through dialogue and negotiation. In cases where external partners, such as government agencies or vendors, played a critical role, managers invested time in building trust and aligning interests.

5. Navigating Resource Constraints

Resource limitations were a constant challenge in the Eastern Caribbean. Managers learned to be resourceful, prioritizing initiatives with the highest impact and seeking creative solutions to funding gaps. This often involved leveraging partnerships, applying for grants, or repurposing existing assets. Managers also advocated for phased implementation approaches, allowing organizations to realize benefits incrementally and build momentum over time.

Theoretical Foundations: Applying the Technology Acceptance Model (TAM)

A distinctive feature of the thesis is its grounding in the Technology Acceptance Model (TAM). Regional IT managers implicitly or explicitly drew on TAM principles to guide their leadership strategies. They recognized that user acceptance depended on two key perceptions: usefulness and ease of use.

To enhance perceived usefulness, managers linked ICT initiatives to concrete improvements in job performance and organizational outcomes. They shared success stories, highlighted measurable benefits, and involved users in defining requirements.

To improve perceived ease of use, managers invested in user-friendly technologies, comprehensive training, and responsive support systems. They sought regular feedback from end-users and made iterative adjustments to ensure that systems were intuitive and accessible.

Overcoming Regional Challenges: Lessons for the Caribbean and Beyond

The experiences of regional IT managers in the Eastern Caribbean offer valuable lessons for leaders operating in similar contexts:

- **Cultural Sensitivity**: Leaders must be attuned to local norms, values, and communication styles. This includes respecting hierarchical structures, leveraging community leaders, and adapting global best practices to local realities.
- **Inclusivity**: Successful ICT projects are those that involve diverse stakeholders from the outset, ensuring that solutions are relevant, equitable, and widely supported.
- **Long-term Commitment**: Digital transformation is a journey, not a destination. Leaders must be prepared for setbacks and maintain a focus on continuous improvement.
- **Knowledge Sharing**: Regional collaboration and peer learning are powerful tools for overcoming resource constraints and building collective capacity.

Implications for Social and Economic Development

The leadership lessons distilled from the thesis have implications that extend beyond organizational boundaries. By guiding successful ICT adoption, regional IT managers contribute to broader goals of social and economic development. These include:

- Lowering barriers to entrepreneurship and innovation
- Expanding access to e-learning and digital services
- Enhancing public sector efficiency and transparency
- Empowering citizens and communities.

Actionable Recommendations

Drawing from the insights gained through the examination of organizational culture, change management, and leadership lessons, several actionable recommendations emerge for organizations seeking to succeed in ICT adoption—particularly within the unique context of the Eastern Caribbean. These recommendations are informed by both the empirical findings of the thesis and the broader theoretical framework of the Technology Acceptance Model (TAM), which emphasizes the importance of perceived usefulness and ease of use in driving technology adoption.

1. Develop a Comprehensive Leadership Strategy Focused on Culture Change

A recurring theme in the research is the critical role of leadership in shaping organizational culture and driving successful ICT integration. Organizations must develop a comprehensive leadership strategy that explicitly prioritizes culture change as a central pillar of digital transformation. This strategy should:

- Define and communicate a clear vision for ICT adoption, linking technology initiatives to tangible business and societal outcomes.
- Model desired behaviors at all levels of leadership, ensuring that senior executives, middle managers, and team leads consistently reinforce the values and practices necessary for digital transformation.
- Invest in leadership development programs that equip managers with the skills needed to lead change, including emotional intelligence, adaptive leadership, and cross-cultural competence.
- Encourage distributed leadership, empowering individuals at all levels to take ownership of ICT initiatives and contribute to the change process.

By embedding culture change into the leadership agenda, organizations can create an environment where innovation, collaboration, and continuous learning are not just encouraged but expected.

2. Implement a Structured yet Flexible Change Management Framework

The thesis findings highlight the need for a structured change management framework that provides clear guidance while remaining adaptable to different organizational units and regional contexts. Such a framework should incorporate the following phases:

- **Advising**: Begin with a thorough assessment of organizational readiness, including technological infrastructure, staff competencies, and cultural attitudes. Use surveys, interviews, and focus groups to surface potential barriers and opportunities.
- **Planning**: Develop a detailed roadmap that outlines objectives, milestones, resource allocation, and communication strategies. Engage stakeholders early and often to ensure buy-in and shared ownership.
- **Transformation**: Execute the change plan with an emphasis on training, support, and iterative feedback. Customize interventions to address the specific needs of different user groups and departments.
- **Feedback and Adjustment**: Establish mechanisms for ongoing monitoring, evaluation, and refinement. Use performance data, user feedback, and lessons learned to adapt strategies in real time.

This approach ensures that change management is systematic and evidence-based, while also being responsive to the dynamic realities of ICT projects in the Caribbean.

3. Ensure Active and Visible Engagement of Leaders

Active engagement of leaders is a critical success factor for ICT adoption. The research demonstrates that when senior executives and regional managers visibly support ICT initiatives—by participating in training, leading communications, and making key decisions—they send a powerful signal about the importance of the change. To operationalize this:

- Leaders should participate in training sessions and workshops alongside staff, demonstrating a commitment to learning and adaptation.
- Regularly communicate progress, challenges, and successes through multiple channels, including town halls, newsletters, and informal gatherings.
- Solicit and respond to feedback from employees at all levels, showing that leadership is attentive and responsive to concerns.
- Recognize and celebrate the contributions of individuals and teams who exemplify the desired behaviors and outcomes.

Visible leadership not only motivates employees but also helps to overcome resistance and build momentum for change.

4. Prioritize Continuous Training and Professional Development

The importance of ongoing training cannot be overstated. The thesis emphasizes that one-off training events are insufficient for building the skills and confidence required for sustained ICT adoption. Instead, organizations should:

- Design training programs that are continuous, modular, and tailored to the specific needs of different user groups (e.g., frontline staff, managers, technical specialists).
- Incorporate a variety of learning modalities, such as hands-on workshops, e-learning modules, peer mentoring, and communities of practice.
- Encourage peer-to-peer learning and knowledge sharing, leveraging the expertise and experience of early adopters and internal champions.
- Evaluate training effectiveness through regular assessments, feedback surveys, and performance metrics, making adjustments as needed.

By investing in professional development, organizations can build a workforce that is adaptable, confident, and capable of leveraging new technologies to drive organizational goals.

5. Promote Open and Transparent Communication

Open and transparent communication is essential for building trust, managing expectations, and fostering a sense of ownership among employees. Organizations should:

- Establish two-way channels for feedback, questions, and concerns, such as suggestion boxes, online forums, and regular Q&A sessions.

- Communicate the rationale, benefits, and progress of ICT initiatives clearly and consistently, addressing both the technical and human aspects of change.
- Celebrate milestones and recognize individual and team achievements throughout the adoption process, reinforcing positive behaviors and sustaining engagement.
- Be transparent about challenges and setbacks, framing them as opportunities for learning and improvement rather than failures.

Transparent communication helps to demystify technology, reduce anxiety, and create a culture where employees feel informed and empowered to contribute.

6. Foster a Supportive and Inclusive Organizational Culture

A supportive and inclusive culture is paramount for successful ICT adoption. The research underscores the importance of creating environments where employees feel valued, safe to innovate, and empowered to contribute. To achieve this:

- Promote diversity and inclusion by ensuring that teams represent a range of perspectives, backgrounds, and experiences.
- Encourage collaboration across departments and regions, breaking down silos and facilitating the sharing of ideas and best practices.

- Cultivate psychological safety, where employees can voice concerns, propose new ideas, and take calculated risks without fear of reprisal.
- Provide recognition and rewards for behaviors that align with organizational values, such as innovation, teamwork, and adaptability.

Such a culture not only supports ICT adoption but also drives broader organizational resilience and performance.

7. Monitor Progress and Adjust Strategies Based on Data

Continuous evaluation is vital for ensuring that ICT adoption remains aligned with strategic goals and delivers the intended benefits. Organizations should:

- Define clear metrics and key performance indicators (KPIs) for ICT adoption, such as user adoption rates, satisfaction scores, and operational improvements.
- Implement regular monitoring and reporting mechanisms, using dashboards, scorecards, and progress reviews to track performance.
- Solicit feedback from end-users and stakeholders, using surveys, interviews, and focus groups to identify emerging challenges and opportunities.
- Be prepared to adjust strategies and interventions based on data and feedback, embracing an agile and iterative approach to change management.

This commitment to continuous improvement ensures that organizations remain responsive to changing conditions and can sustain momentum over the long term.

Integrating Recommendations with Regional Realities

The recommendations above are grounded in the specific context of the Eastern Caribbean, where organizations face unique challenges and opportunities in ICT adoption. The thesis identifies several contextual factors that should inform the implementation of these recommendations:

- **Resource Constraints**: Many organizations operate with limited budgets and technical capacity. Prioritizing high-impact initiatives, leveraging partnerships, and seeking external funding (e.g., grants, regional collaborations) can help to overcome these constraints.
- **Cultural Diversity**: The Caribbean is characterized by diverse cultures, languages, and organizational norms. Tailoring change management strategies to local contexts, respecting cultural differences, and engaging community leaders can enhance buy-in and effectiveness.
- **Government and Regulatory Environment**: Public sector organizations must navigate complex regulatory frameworks and stakeholder landscapes. Building strong relationships with government agencies, aligning ICT initiatives with national

strategies, and advocating for enabling policies are critical for success.

- **Rapid Technological Change**: The pace of technological innovation requires organizations to be agile and forward-looking. Investing in continuous learning, fostering a culture of experimentation, and staying abreast of global trends are essential for maintaining competitiveness.

Building an IT Implementation Framework

A key recommendation from the thesis is the development of an IT implementation framework that aligns with established project management methodologies (such as the Project Management Body of Knowledge, PMBOK) and incorporates remedial measures to achieve defined project objectives. This framework should:

- Integrate change management principles into every phase of the project lifecycle, from initiation to closure.
- Embed mechanisms for stakeholder engagement, risk management, and quality assurance, ensuring that projects are delivered on time, within budget, and to the required standard.
- Facilitate knowledge sharing and documentation, capturing lessons learned and best practices for future initiatives.
- Support scalability and sustainability, enabling organizations to build on initial successes and expand ICT adoption over time.

Such a framework provides a structured yet flexible approach to managing the complexity of ICT projects, increasing the likelihood of successful outcomes.

Implications for Social and Economic Development

The successful adoption of ICT has implications that extend far beyond individual organizations. As highlighted in the thesis, effective ICT integration can:

- Lower barriers to starting and growing businesses
- Enable e-commerce, online learning, and digital innovation
- Improve public service delivery and transparency
- Empower citizens and communities
- Enhance regional competitiveness in the global digital economy

By implementing the actionable recommendations outlined above, organizations can contribute to positive social change and help build a more inclusive, prosperous, and resilient digital future for the Eastern Caribbean and beyond.

Conclusion

The journey toward successful ICT adoption is complex and multifaceted, requiring a holistic approach that integrates leadership, culture, change management, and continuous learning. The actionable recommendations presented here—rooted in empirical research and tailored to the realities of the Eastern Caribbean—provide a roadmap for organizations seeking to harness the transformative power of technology.

By developing comprehensive leadership strategies, implementing structured change management frameworks, engaging leaders and stakeholders, prioritizing training, fostering inclusive cultures, and continuously monitoring progress, organizations can build the resilience and capabilities needed to thrive in the digital age. The lessons and strategies distilled from the experiences of IT project managers in the region offer valuable guidance not only for the Caribbean but for any organization navigating the challenges and opportunities of digital transformation

Chapter 5

Navigating Government Networks and Policies

Introduction

The integration of information and communication technologies (ICTs) across the Caribbean, and particularly in the Eastern Caribbean, is inseparable from the influence and actions of government. Governments serve as both a springboard and, at times, a stumbling block for ICT adoption and transformation. Their policies, regulatory environments, and willingness to collaborate with public and private sector partners shape the pace and success of digital transformation efforts. Understanding how to navigate these government networks and policies is essential for any organization or individual seeking to implement or expand ICT initiatives in the region.

The Central Role of Government in ICT Integration

Government involvement in ICT is multifaceted, encompassing policy development, regulatory oversight, infrastructure investment, and direct participation in project implementation. In the Eastern Caribbean, governments are often the primary drivers of large-scale ICT initiatives, such as national broadband networks, e-government platforms, and public sector digitalization. This central role arises from the need for coordinated action across ministries and agencies, the scale of investment required, and the strategic importance of ICT for national development.

Government policy can be a powerful catalyst for ICT integration. Well-crafted policies provide direction, set priorities, allocate resources, and establish standards that guide both public and private sector actors. For example, the adoption of national ICT strategies and e-government frameworks has enabled Eastern Caribbean states to pursue ambitious projects like the Caribbean Regional Communications Infrastructure Program (CARCIP), which aims to expand broadband access and foster digital innovation. However, policy can also act as a constraint. Outdated regulations, bureaucratic inertia, and fragmented governance structures can slow progress and create uncertainty for stakeholders. The absence of clear policies on issues such as data privacy, cybersecurity, and procurement can deter investment and hinder the adoption of new technologies. Thus, navigating the policy landscape requires both awareness of existing frameworks and the agility to respond to evolving regulatory requirements.

Organizational Structures and Decision-Making

A defining feature of ICT integration in the Eastern Caribbean is the organizational structure through which government manages digital initiatives. Effective management of organizational structure is essential for aligning ICT projects with national development goals and ensuring coordination across ministries, agencies, and external partners. Many successful ICT projects in the region are guided by high-level steering committees composed of representatives from key ministries, technical experts, and sometimes private sector stakeholders. These committees provide strategic oversight, facilitate inter-ministerial coordination, and ensure that projects remain aligned with broader government objectives. For example, the establishment of a steering committee for CARCIP enabled the harmonization of infrastructure investments, regulatory reforms, and capacity-building efforts across multiple countries.

There is often a tension between centralization and decentralization in the management of ICT initiatives. Centralized structures, such as a dedicated Ministry of ICT or a national ICT authority, can provide clear leadership, standardize processes, and streamline decision-making. Decentralized approaches, on the other hand, may empower individual ministries or agencies to tailor solutions to their specific needs but risk fragmentation and duplication of effort. The most effective models balance these approaches, centralizing policy and strategy while decentralizing implementation to leverage local expertise and context.

Policy Development and Legal Frameworks

The legal and policy environment is a critical determinant of ICT project success. Governments in the Eastern Caribbean have made significant strides in developing comprehensive ICT policies, e-government strategies, and regulatory frameworks to support digital transformation. National ICT strategies articulate a vision for digital development, set targets for infrastructure deployment, and outline priorities for e-government, education, health, and business. These strategies are typically developed through consultative processes involving government, industry, and civil society, ensuring that they reflect diverse perspectives and needs. In Grenada and St. Vincent and the Grenadines, for example, national ICT strategies have prioritized broadband expansion, digital literacy, and the creation of enabling environments for innovation.

Regulatory reform is essential for fostering competition, protecting consumers, and ensuring the security and reliability of ICT services. Key areas of focus include telecommunications regulation, liberalizing markets, licensing new entrants, and promoting infrastructure sharing. Data protection and privacy laws are enacted to safeguard personal data and build public trust in digital services. Cybersecurity strategies are developed, incident response teams established, and collaboration with international partners is pursued. Standardizing procurement processes and technical standards ensures interoperability and value for money. Despite progress, legislative gaps and delays can impede ICT integration. For instance, the slow passage of e-government and data protection laws can create uncertainty for project implementers and users alike. Furthermore, legal frameworks must be regularly updated to keep pace with technological change and emerging risks.

Government Networks: Infrastructure and Implementation

The physical and digital infrastructure underpinning ICT integration is often developed and managed through government-led networks and partnerships. These networks are foundational to the delivery of e-government services, digital education, and business innovation. A pivotal initiative in the Eastern Caribbean has been the implementation of government wide area networks (GWANs), which connect government offices, schools, and public institutions via high-speed fiber-optic infrastructure. These networks serve as the backbone for e-government services, enabling secure data sharing, unified communications, and the rollout of digital platforms across multiple sectors.

The CARCIP project, for example, involved the deployment of hundreds of kilometers of subsea and terrestrial fiber-optic cable, linking islands and facilitating regional integration. GWANs are typically managed by a central government agency or in partnership with private telecommunications providers, ensuring both public oversight and operational efficiency. E-government platforms are at the heart of digital transformation efforts, providing citizens and businesses with online access to government services such as tax filing, business registration, and social welfare applications. The success of these platforms depends on robust infrastructure, user-friendly design, and supportive policies that encourage adoption and trust.

Given the scale and complexity of ICT infrastructure projects, governments often engage in public-private partnerships (PPPs) to leverage private sector expertise, investment, and innovation. PPPs can accelerate project delivery, share risks, and ensure the sustainability of digital services. However, effective PPPs require clear legal frameworks, transparent procurement processes, and mechanisms for accountability and performance monitoring.

Navigating Budgetary and Resource Constraints

Financing ICT projects is a persistent challenge for governments in the Eastern Caribbean, given limited fiscal space and competing development priorities. Budgetary constraints can delay project implementation, limit the scope of initiatives, and affect the sustainability of digital services. To overcome resource limitations, governments frequently seek funding and technical assistance from international donors such as the World Bank, Inter-American Development Bank, and bilateral partners. Donor-funded projects often come with requirements for transparency, results-based management, and alignment with national development strategies. Navigating these requirements demands strong project management capabilities and the ability to coordinate across multiple stakeholders.

Sustainable ICT integration requires investment not only in technology but also in human capital. Governments must prioritize training and capacity-building for public sector employees, IT professionals, and end-users to ensure that new systems are effectively adopted and maintained. This includes developing digital literacy programs, supporting professional development, and fostering a culture of continuous learning and innovation.

Overcoming Barriers: Buy-In, Change Management, and Culture

Even the best-designed policies and networks can falter without the buy-in of key stakeholders and the broader public. Resistance to change, cultural inertia, and lack of awareness can undermine ICT initiatives. Early and continuous engagement with stakeholders—including government employees, private sector partners, civil society, and end-users—is essential for building support and addressing concerns. Strategies for stakeholder engagement include conducting needs assessments and consultations during project design, providing clear communication about project goals, benefits, and impacts, involving users in pilot testing and feedback processes, and recognizing and rewarding contributions to project success.

Successful ICT integration requires deliberate change management strategies to guide organizations and individuals through transitions. This involves training and capacity-building to develop new skills and competencies, leadership support to champion change and model desired behaviors, addressing fears about job loss or increased workload through transparent communication and support, and monitoring and evaluating progress to identify challenges and adapt strategies as needed. Ultimately, the long-term success of ICT initiatives depends on cultivating a culture that values innovation, collaboration, and continuous improvement. Governments can lead by example, promoting digital literacy, supporting experimentation, and creating environments where new ideas are encouraged and rewarded.

Lessons Learned and Recommendations

The experience of ICT integration in the Eastern Caribbean offers several lessons for navigating government networks and policies. Strategic alignment is crucial: ICT initiatives must be aligned with national development goals and supported by high-level leadership. Comprehensive policy frameworks should be developed and regularly updated to address emerging challenges and opportunities. Effective organizational structures are needed, with clear roles, responsibilities, and coordination mechanisms to manage complex projects. Stakeholder engagement should be prioritized from the outset to build buy-in and address concerns. Investment in human capital is essential to support the adoption and sustainability of digital initiatives. Resource mobilization through donor funding, PPPs, and innovative financing mechanisms can help overcome budgetary constraints. Finally, implementing strategies to manage resistance and foster a culture of innovation is necessary for successful change management.

Navigating government networks and policies is a complex but essential aspect of ICT integration in the Eastern

Caribbean. Governments play a decisive role in shaping the digital landscape through their policies, organizational structures, and investment decisions. By understanding and engaging with these dynamics, organizations and individuals can more effectively implement and expand ICT initiatives, contributing to the region's digital transformation and socio-economic development.

The Role of Government in Enabling (or Hindering) ICT Integration

Government involvement in ICT integration is multifaceted. On one hand, governments can be powerful enablers, setting the vision and providing the infrastructure necessary for digital advancement. In countries like Grenada and St. Vincent and the Grenadines, the government's recognition of ICT as a driver for economic growth, public sector efficiency, and social development has led to the creation of national ICT strategies. These strategies articulate clear goals for digital transformation, such as expanding broadband access, digitizing government services, and integrating ICT into education. By investing in foundational infrastructure like government-wide area networks (GWANs) and subsea fiber-optic cables, governments lay the groundwork for both public sector innovation and private sector growth.

Moreover, governments play a critical role in fostering digital literacy and capacity building. Through training programs and educational reforms, they ensure that both public sector employees and citizens are equipped to use new technologies effectively. These efforts are vital in overcoming the digital divide and ensuring that the benefits of ICT integration are widely distributed. The government's support for innovation ecosystems, including the encouragement of research, entrepreneurship, and public-private partnerships, further stimulates the development of local ICT industries.

However, the same governments that enable ICT integration can also inadvertently hinder progress. Bureaucratic inertia, characterized by slow approval processes and rigid procurement systems, often delays project implementation and stifles innovation. Fragmented policy approaches, where ministries and agencies operate in silos without adequate coordination, can lead to duplicated efforts, incompatible systems, and wasted resources. Resistance to change is another significant barrier, especially among public sector employees who may fear job displacement or lack the necessary skills to adapt to new technologies. The absence of up-to-date legal and regulatory frameworks further complicates matters, as laws may lag behind technological advancements, leaving issues like data privacy, cyber security, and system interoperability inadequately addressed.

The duality of government's role—both as an enabler and a potential obstacle—reflects the complex realities of public sector management in the Caribbean. On the enabling side, visionary leadership at the highest levels often makes the difference between stagnation and progress. When heads of government and senior officials champion digital transformation, they send a strong signal to ministries, agencies, and the private sector that ICT is a national priority. This leadership is reflected in the allocation of budgetary resources for ICT infrastructure, the establishment of dedicated ICT ministries or departments, and the integration of digital goals into national development plans.

In Grenada, for example, the government's commitment to ICT is evident in its sustained efforts to expand broadband connectivity and modernize public services. The implementation of a government-wide area network has enabled secure, high-speed communication between ministries, improved data sharing, and facilitated the rollout of e-government services. Similarly, St. Vincent and the Grenadines has invested in subsea fiber-optic infrastructure, connecting the country to regional and global networks and laying the foundation for digital innovation across sectors.

The impact of these investments is far-reaching. Enhanced connectivity supports not only government operations but also the private sector, enabling businesses to access new markets, adopt cloud-based solutions, and participate in the digital economy. In education, improved infrastructure allows schools to integrate digital learning tools, expanding opportunities for students and teachers alike. In health, telemedicine and electronic health records become feasible, improving access to care and the efficiency of service delivery.

Government involvement extends beyond infrastructure to the creation of enabling environments for innovation. By fostering public-private partnerships, governments can leverage private sector expertise, investment, and agility. These partnerships are particularly important in small island developing states, where limited resources and technical capacity can constrain the scale and scope of public sector initiatives. Through collaboration, governments and private companies can co-develop solutions, share risks, and accelerate the pace of digital transformation.

Capacity building is another area where government leadership is essential. The rapid evolution of technology requires a workforce that is adaptable, digitally literate, and capable of managing complex ICT systems. Governments in the Eastern Caribbean have responded by investing in training programs for public sector employees, integrating ICT into school curricula, and supporting initiatives that promote digital literacy among citizens. These efforts help to ensure that the benefits of ICT are accessible to all, reducing inequalities and promoting inclusive development.

Despite these positive developments, significant challenges remain. Bureaucratic inertia is a persistent problem, particularly in environments where decision-making processes are slow and hierarchical. The approval of ICT projects may be delayed by lengthy procurement procedures, multiple layers of review, and a reluctance to deviate from established practices. This inertia can be exacerbated by a lack of technical understanding among senior officials, leading to risk aversion and a preference for the status quo.

Fragmentation of policy and governance structures is another barrier to effective ICT integration. In many cases, responsibility for digital initiatives is spread across multiple ministries and agencies, each with its own priorities, budgets, and mandates. Without effective coordination, this can result in duplicated efforts, incompatible systems, and missed opportunities for synergy. For example, one ministry may invest in a digital platform that cannot interface with systems used by other agencies, undermining the potential for integrated service delivery.

Resistance to change is a human factor that cannot be overlooked. The introduction of new technologies often disrupts established workflows, requiring employees to acquire new skills and adapt to different ways of working. Some public sector workers may fear that automation and digitalization will lead to job losses or diminished roles. Others may lack confidence in their ability to use new systems effectively. Addressing these concerns requires not only technical training but also clear communication about the benefits of digital transformation and the opportunities it creates for professional growth.

Legal and regulatory frameworks are critical to the success of ICT integration, yet they often lag behind technological change. The rapid pace of innovation in areas such as cloud computing, cyber security, and data analytics creates challenges for policymakers, who must balance the need for flexibility with the imperative to protect citizens' rights and interests. In the absence of up-to-date laws, issues such as data privacy, cyber security, and system interoperability may be inadequately addressed, exposing governments and citizens to risks.

The experience of the Eastern Caribbean highlights the importance of ongoing policy review and adaptation. Governments must be proactive in updating legal frameworks to reflect emerging technologies and evolving threats. This includes enacting data protection laws that safeguard personal information, developing cyber security strategies that address both prevention and response, and establishing standards for system interoperability to ensure that digital platforms can communicate effectively.

Budgetary constraints are a further challenge for governments in the region. The development and maintenance of ICT infrastructure require significant investment, yet fiscal space is often limited. Competing priorities—such as health, education, and infrastructure—can make it difficult to allocate sufficient resources to digital initiatives. To address this, governments have increasingly turned to international donors, development banks, and public-private partnerships to mobilize funding and technical assistance. While external support can be invaluable, it also comes with expectations of transparency, accountability, and alignment with broader development goals.

The management of organizational structure is another key factor influencing the success of ICT integration. Effective project management requires clear roles and responsibilities, strong leadership, and mechanisms for coordination and accountability. In the Eastern Caribbean, the establishment of steering committees and inter-ministerial working groups has proven effective in guiding complex digital initiatives. These bodies bring together representatives from key ministries, technical experts, and sometimes private sector partners, providing strategic oversight and facilitating collaboration.

At the same time, there is a need to balance centralization and decentralization in the management of ICT projects. Centralized structures, such as dedicated ICT ministries or authorities, can provide clear leadership and standardize processes. However, decentralization may empower individual ministries or agencies to tailor solutions to their specific needs and contexts. The most effective models strike a balance, centralizing policy and strategy while decentralizing implementation to leverage local expertise and foster innovation.

Change management is an essential component of successful ICT integration. The introduction of new technologies is not merely a technical exercise; it is a process of organizational transformation that requires buy-in from all stakeholders. Governments must invest in communication, training, and support to help employees navigate the transition, addressing concerns about job security and workload. Celebrating early successes and recognizing the contributions of individuals and teams can help to build momentum and sustain commitment.

The cultivation of a digital culture within government is equally important. This involves fostering an environment that values innovation, experimentation, and continuous learning. Leaders can set the tone by promoting digital literacy, encouraging the sharing of ideas, and supporting pilot projects that test new approaches. Over time, the development of a digital mindset can help to overcome resistance and create a foundation for ongoing transformation.

In conclusion, the role of government in ICT integration in the Eastern Caribbean is both enabling and constraining. Visionary leadership, investment in infrastructure, support for capacity building, and the creation of enabling environments for innovation are critical drivers of progress. At the same time, bureaucratic inertia, fragmented governance, resistance to change, outdated legal frameworks, and budgetary constraints pose significant challenges. The experience of countries like Grenada and St. Vincent and the Grenadines demonstrates that success depends on the ability to navigate these complexities, adapt to changing circumstances, and maintain a clear focus on the ultimate goal: harnessing the power of ICT to drive economic growth, improve public services, and promote social development. As governments continue to evolve in their approach to digital transformation, ongoing collaboration, learning, and adaptation will be essential to realizing the full potential of ICT for the region and its people.

Policy Frameworks and Regulatory Environments

The development and implementation of robust policy frameworks are fundamental to the successful integration of information and communication technologies (ICTs) in the Caribbean. In the context of the Eastern Caribbean, these frameworks serve as the backbone for digital transformation, providing both a strategic vision and practical mechanisms for execution. Effective ICT policy frameworks are characterized not only by their clarity of purpose but also by their ability to establish comprehensive governance structures. These structures are vital for overseeing and coordinating the multitude of activities required for ICT integration, ensuring that efforts are aligned across government ministries, agencies, and even regional partners.

A well-crafted policy framework sets the standards and guidelines necessary to guarantee that ICT systems are interoperable, secure, and of high quality. This is particularly important in small island developing states, where resources are limited and the risks of fragmentation and duplication are high. By mandating interoperability and security standards, governments can avoid the pitfalls of isolated systems that cannot communicate with one another, thereby maximizing the value of public investments in technology. Furthermore, these frameworks provide for mechanisms of monitoring and evaluation, which enable governments to track progress, assess the impact of ICT initiatives, and make evidence-based adjustments as circumstances evolve. This iterative approach is essential in a rapidly changing technological landscape, where static policies can quickly become obsolete.

The regulatory environment, which operates alongside the policy framework, shapes the incentives and constraints faced by both public and private actors in the ICT sector. Telecommunications regulation is a prime example of how regulatory choices can either enable or impede digital progress. Regulations that promote competition among service providers tend to drive down prices, increase service quality, and expand access to broadband infrastructure. Conversely, overly restrictive or monopolistic regulatory environments can stifle innovation and limit the reach of digital services. In the Eastern Caribbean, efforts to liberalize the telecommunications sector have yielded significant benefits, but challenges remain in ensuring universal access and affordability, particularly in rural and underserved communities.

Data protection and privacy laws are increasingly recognized as critical components of the regulatory environment. As governments and businesses collect and process vast amounts of personal information through digital platforms, the need to safeguard citizens' privacy becomes paramount. Robust data protection laws help to build public trust in digital services, encouraging greater uptake and participation in e-government initiatives. In the absence of such protections, citizens may be reluctant to engage with online platforms, undermining the effectiveness of digital transformation efforts. The thesis by

Carl S. Roberts emphasizes that the lack of comprehensive data privacy frameworks in some Eastern Caribbean countries has been a source of concern, highlighting the need for ongoing legislative reform.

Procurement policies also play a significant role in shaping the ICT landscape. Flexible and transparent procurement processes are necessary to allow governments to acquire the latest technologies and services in a timely manner. Rigid or opaque procurement systems can result in delays, cost overruns, and the selection of suboptimal solutions. In the context of ICT, where technological advances occur rapidly, the ability to adapt procurement practices is especially important. Governments must strike a balance between ensuring accountability and enabling agility, so that they can respond effectively to emerging needs and opportunities.

Regulations that promote open government, citizen engagement, and the use of open data can further enhance the legitimacy and effectiveness of ICT initiatives. Open government policies encourage transparency and accountability, making it easier for citizens to access information, participate in decision-making, and hold public officials to account. The use of open data—where government datasets are made freely available for public use—can spur innovation, support research, and empower civil society organizations to contribute to the policy process. In the Eastern Caribbean, some governments have begun to embrace open data principles, but progress is uneven and further efforts are needed to realize the full potential of these approaches.

Despite the recognized importance of robust policy frameworks and regulatory environments, Caribbean governments face significant challenges in their development and enforcement. Resource constraints are a persistent issue, affecting both the financial and human capacity available for policy design and implementation. Small states often lack the technical expertise required to draft complex legislation, manage regulatory processes, and oversee compliance. This can lead to reliance on external consultants or international organizations, which, while helpful, may not always be fully attuned to local contexts and needs.

Efforts to harmonize policies across the region, such as through CARICOM's Single ICT Space initiative, are further complicated by differences in capacity, political will, and economic development among member states. While regional harmonization offers the promise of greater efficiency and coherence, it also requires significant coordination and compromise. Countries at different stages of digital development may have divergent priorities, making it difficult to agree on common standards and approaches. The thesis notes that while regional initiatives have provided valuable frameworks for collaboration, implementation on the ground often lags due to these contextual differences.

The rapid pace of technological change presents another formidable challenge. Legal and regulatory frameworks, by their nature, tend to lag behind technological innovation. New developments in areas such as cloud computing, artificial intelligence, and cybersecurity can quickly render existing laws outdated or inadequate. This creates gaps and uncertainties that can undermine ICT integration, as both public and private actors may be unsure about their rights, responsibilities, and the risks involved. The need for ongoing policy review and adaptation is therefore paramount. Governments must be proactive in updating their frameworks to keep pace with emerging technologies, while also ensuring that fundamental principles—such as privacy, security, and interoperability—are upheld.

The thesis by Roberts also highlights the importance of stakeholder engagement in the policy development process. Effective frameworks are those that are informed by the perspectives and needs of a wide range of stakeholders, including government officials, private sector representatives, civil society organizations, and end-users. Inclusive consultation processes help to ensure that policies are realistic, relevant, and capable of garnering broad-based support. They also provide an opportunity to identify potential barriers to implementation and to design strategies for overcoming them. In the Eastern Caribbean, experiences with stakeholder engagement have been mixed, with some countries demonstrating strong participatory approaches and others relying more heavily on top-down decision-making.

Monitoring and evaluation are integral to the success of policy frameworks and regulatory environments. Without effective mechanisms for tracking progress and assessing impact, it is difficult for governments to know whether their ICT initiatives are achieving their intended outcomes. Regular monitoring allows for the identification of problems and the adjustment of strategies as needed, ensuring that resources are used efficiently and that benefits are maximized. Evaluation also provides valuable evidence for future policy development, helping to build a culture of learning and continuous improvement.

In practice, the implementation of policy frameworks and regulatory environments is often shaped by broader political and institutional factors. Leadership at the highest levels is crucial for setting priorities, mobilizing resources, and driving change. Where political will is strong, progress tends to be more rapid and sustained. Conversely, where leadership is lacking or fragmented, ICT integration efforts may stall. Institutional arrangements—such as the existence of dedicated ICT ministries or agencies—can also influence the effectiveness of policy implementation. Centralized structures may provide clearer direction and coordination, while decentralized approaches may allow for greater flexibility and responsiveness to local needs.

The experience of the Eastern Caribbean demonstrates that there is no one-size-fits-all approach to policy and regulation. Each country must navigate its own unique set of challenges and opportunities, drawing on regional and international best practices while adapting them to local circumstances. The most successful frameworks are those that are dynamic and responsive, capable of evolving in response to new developments and emerging risks. They are also those that are grounded in a clear understanding of the local context, informed by robust data and evidence, and supported by strong institutions and leadership.

Ultimately, the goal of policy frameworks and regulatory environments in the ICT sector is to create conditions that enable innovation, inclusion, and sustainable development. This requires a delicate balance between promoting competition and protecting the public interest, between enabling rapid technological adoption and safeguarding fundamental rights. In the Caribbean, as elsewhere, the stakes are high. The effective integration of ICTs has the potential to transform economies, improve public services, and enhance the quality of life for all citizens. Achieving this potential depends on the ability of governments to develop and enforce policies and regulations that are fit for purpose, forward-looking, and inclusive.

The journey toward robust policy frameworks and regulatory environments is ongoing. It demands not only technical expertise and financial resources but also vision, leadership, and a commitment to collaboration. As the digital landscape continues to evolve, Caribbean governments must remain vigilant, adaptable, and open to new ideas. By doing so, they can ensure that their countries are well-positioned to harness the benefits of ICT and to navigate the challenges of an increasingly digital world.

Collaborating with Public Sector Partners

Collaboration among public sector partners is an indispensable element in the successful integration of information and communication technologies (ICTs) within the Caribbean, especially in the context of the Eastern Caribbean. The very nature of digital transformation dictates that technology initiatives rarely exist in isolation;

rather, they cut across the boundaries of ministries, agencies, and public institutions. This cross-cutting reality means that no single entity can achieve digital transformation on its own. Instead, a collective approach, built on robust collaboration, is required to ensure that ICT projects are not only implemented effectively but also sustained and scaled for long-term impact.

At the foundation of this collaborative spirit is the recognition that the challenges and opportunities posed by ICT integration are shared. Ministries of education, health, finance, national security, and other sectors all depend on digital platforms to deliver their services, manage data, and communicate with citizens. The interdependence of these entities becomes even more pronounced as governments seek to modernize their operations through e-government initiatives, digital records management, and integrated service delivery. The thesis by Carl S. Roberts underscores that successful ICT integration is often a function of how well these diverse actors work together, share information, and align their efforts toward common goals.

One of the most effective ways to foster collaboration is through the establishment of structured, formal mechanisms that facilitate coordination and joint decision-making. Steering committees, for example, are frequently used to bring together representatives from key ministries, technical experts, and sometimes private sector partners. These committees serve as a central forum for discussing project objectives, monitoring progress, and resolving challenges as they arise. By providing a platform where all voices can be heard and where decisions are made collectively, steering committees help to break down the silos that often exist within government. The presence of a high-level steering committee can also signal the importance of the initiative, ensuring that it receives the attention and resources needed from across the public sector.

Technical working groups play a complementary role, focusing on the operational details of ICT projects. These groups typically include IT professionals, project managers, and subject matter experts who are responsible for translating strategic objectives into actionable plans. Their work often involves developing technical specifications, setting interoperability standards, and troubleshooting implementation issues. By pooling expertise from different agencies, technical working groups can draw on a wide range of experiences and perspectives, leading to more robust and innovative solutions.

Cabinet-level coordination bodies represent another layer of collaboration, particularly for initiatives that have far-reaching policy implications or require significant resource allocation. When digital transformation is championed at the highest levels of government, it sends a clear message that ICT is a national priority. Cabinet-level engagement can help to overcome bureaucratic inertia, resolve inter-ministerial disputes, and ensure that digital initiatives are aligned with broader development strategies. In the Eastern Caribbean, the involvement of cabinet-level bodies has been instrumental in advancing large-scale projects such as government-wide area networks (GWANs) and national broadband strategies.

Beyond formal structures, the process of collaboration is greatly enhanced by inclusive planning processes. Engaging all relevant stakeholders—including not only government officials but also end-users, civil society organizations, and the private sector—from the outset creates a sense of shared ownership and responsibility. When stakeholders are involved in defining project objectives, identifying requirements, and designing solutions, they are more likely to support the initiative and less likely to resist change. This participatory approach also helps to surface potential challenges early in the process, allowing for proactive mitigation strategies.

Regular communication is the lifeblood of effective collaboration. In the absence of clear and consistent communication, misunderstandings can arise, progress can stall, and trust can erode. Successful ICT projects in the Eastern Caribbean have often been characterized by frequent meetings, transparent reporting, and open channels for feedback and discussion. Communication is not limited to formal meetings; it also includes informal interactions, updates through digital platforms, and the sharing of best practices and lessons learned. These ongoing exchanges help to build relationships, foster mutual understanding, and keep all partners aligned as projects evolve.

Capacity building is another critical pillar supporting collaboration among public sector partners. The rapid pace of technological change means that continuous learning is essential. Governments must invest in training programs that enhance the technical skills of IT staff, project managers, and end-users alike. Capacity building goes beyond technical training; it also includes developing competencies in project management, change management, and stakeholder engagement. By building a skilled and adaptable workforce, governments can ensure that collaborative structures are not only established but also effective in practice.

The development of clear, documented procedures further underpins successful collaboration. Standard operating procedures, project charters, and memoranda of understanding provide a common reference point for all partners, clarifying roles, responsibilities, and expectations. These documents help to institutionalize collaboration, making it less dependent on individual personalities and more resilient to changes in leadership or staffing. In the Eastern Caribbean, the formalization of procedures has been particularly important in ensuring continuity and accountability in ICT projects, especially given the frequent turnover of public sector personnel.

Despite the many benefits of collaboration, it is not without its challenges. One of the most significant obstacles is the persistence of organizational silos. Ministries and agencies may be reluctant to share information or resources, fearing a loss of autonomy or control. This can lead to duplication of effort, fragmented systems, and missed opportunities for synergy. Overcoming these barriers requires strong leadership, a clear articulation of the benefits of collaboration, and, in some cases, incentives for inter-agency cooperation.

Another challenge lies in balancing the diverse interests and priorities of different stakeholders. While all partners may agree on the importance of digital transformation, their specific objectives, timelines, and resource constraints may differ. Reaching consensus on key decisions can be time-consuming, and there is always the risk that competing agendas will slow progress. Effective facilitation, negotiation skills, and a focus on shared goals are essential for navigating these complexities.

The issue of resource constraints is also ever-present in the context of the Eastern Caribbean. Limited financial and human resources can strain collaborative efforts, particularly when multiple agencies are competing for the same pool of funding or technical expertise. In some cases, external funding from international donors or development partners has been instrumental in bridging resource gaps and enabling joint initiatives. However, reliance on external support also brings its own challenges, including the need to align donor priorities with local needs and to ensure sustainability once funding ends.

The thesis by Roberts highlights several strategies that have proven effective in promoting collaboration among public sector partners. One such strategy is the alignment of ICT initiatives with national development goals. When digital projects are clearly linked to broader economic and social objectives—such as improving education, enhancing healthcare, or promoting economic diversification—they are more likely to receive cross-sectoral support. This alignment also helps to justify the allocation of resources and to sustain political commitment over time.

Another important strategy is the use of pilot projects and phased implementation. By starting with small-scale, well-defined initiatives, governments can demonstrate the value of collaboration, build trust among partners, and generate momentum for larger-scale efforts. Pilot projects provide an opportunity to test new approaches, identify challenges, and refine processes before scaling up. The lessons learned from these early efforts can inform the design of future projects and contribute to a culture of continuous improvement.

The role of leadership cannot be overstated in fostering collaboration. Strong, visionary leaders who are committed to digital transformation can inspire others, break down resistance, and drive change across organizational boundaries. Leadership is needed not only at the top but also at the middle and operational levels, where much of the day-to-day coordination takes place. Investing in leadership development and recognizing the contributions of collaborative champions can help to sustain momentum and embed collaboration as a core value within the public sector.

The integration of ICTs in the Eastern Caribbean has also benefited from regional collaboration. Initiatives such as the Caribbean Regional Communications Infrastructure Program (CARCIP) and efforts to create a Single ICT Space through CARICOM have brought together governments, regional organizations, and development partners to address common challenges and share resources. Regional collaboration enables economies of scale, facilitates knowledge exchange, and strengthens the collective bargaining power of small states in negotiations with technology vendors and service providers.

In addition to regional initiatives, partnerships with the private sector and civil society have enriched the collaborative landscape. Private companies bring technical expertise, innovation, and investment, while civil society organizations provide valuable insights into the needs and perspectives of citizens. By engaging a broad spectrum of partners, governments can tap into a wider pool of resources, ideas, and networks, enhancing the effectiveness and sustainability of ICT projects.

Ultimately, the success of collaboration among public sector partners hinges on a shared vision, mutual trust, and a commitment to collective action. While challenges are inevitable, the experience of the Eastern Caribbean demonstrates that they can be overcome through structured coordination, inclusive planning, regular communication, capacity building, and strong leadership. As governments continue to navigate the complexities of digital transformation, deepening collaboration within the public sector—and beyond—will remain essential to unlocking the full potential of ICTs for national and regional development.

In conclusion, collaboration among public sector partners is not merely a desirable feature of ICT integration; it is a necessity. The complexity of digital transformation demands a coordinated, whole-of-government approach that leverages the strengths of all stakeholders. By building collaborative structures, fostering inclusive planning, investing in capacity building, and institutionalizing clear procedures, governments in the Eastern Caribbean can overcome barriers, maximize synergies, and drive sustainable digital change. The lessons learned from these experiences offer valuable guidance for other regions and countries embarking on similar journeys toward a digitally empowered future.

Case Study: Policy-Driven ICT Transformation in the Eastern Caribbean

A closer look at the experiences of Grenada and St. Vincent and the Grenadines provides a compelling illustration of both the promise and the complexity of policy-driven ICT transformation in small island developing states. These countries have emerged as regional leaders in digital innovation, not because of abundant resources, but because of a deliberate, strategic approach to policy, governance, and collaboration. Their journey highlights the interplay of visionary leadership, comprehensive frameworks, and the persistent challenges that confront governments striving for digital transformation.

The foundation for digital transformation in both Grenada and St. Vincent and the Grenadines has been the articulation of clear national ICT strategies. These strategies, developed through broad consultation and with input from multiple stakeholders, set forth ambitious goals: expanding broadband infrastructure, digitizing government services, integrating ICT into education, and fostering digital literacy across society. The policy frameworks in these countries are not static documents; rather, they are living roadmaps that guide investment, reform, and innovation. They recognize that ICT is not an end in itself, but a catalyst for economic growth, public sector efficiency, and social development.

Central to the success of these strategies has been the prioritization of broadband infrastructure. Both countries have invested heavily in the development of government-wide area networks (GWANs) and the deployment of subsea fiber-optic cables. These investments have dramatically increased the availability and quality of high-speed internet, connecting government offices, schools, hospitals, and even remote communities. The Caribbean Regional Communications Infrastructure Program (CARCIP), supported by multilateral partners, has played a pivotal role in this regard. Through CARCIP, Grenada and St. Vincent and the Grenadines have been able to leverage regional cooperation, pool resources, and adopt best practices from across the Caribbean.

The impact of these infrastructure investments has been transformative. In education, for example, the rollout of the MESH network and the provision of high-speed connectivity to schools have enabled the implementation of e-learning and e-testing initiatives. Students and teachers now have access to a wealth of digital resources, online assessment tools, and collaborative platforms that were previously out of reach. The COVID-19 pandemic underscored the importance of this connectivity, as schools were able to pivot to remote learning with far greater agility than would have been possible otherwise. In the public sector, digitized government services have streamlined processes, reduced paperwork, and made it easier for citizens to access essential services online.

Governance structures have been another cornerstone of policy-driven ICT transformation. Recognizing the cross-cutting nature of digital initiatives, both Grenada and St. Vincent and the Grenadines established centralized ICT ministries tasked with overseeing and coordinating digital policy. These ministries act as hubs for innovation, ensuring that ICT projects align with national priorities and that resources are allocated efficiently. Multi-stakeholder steering and technical committees, comprising representatives from key ministries, technical experts, and sometimes private sector partners, provide additional layers of oversight and coordination. These bodies facilitate information sharing, resolve inter-agency conflicts, and ensure that projects remain on track.

Legal reform has also been a critical enabler of digital transformation. Both countries have enacted legislation to facilitate electronic transactions, protect personal data, and enhance cybersecurity. These laws provide the legal certainty needed to support e-government, e-commerce, and digital innovation. For instance, the enactment of electronic transactions acts has enabled citizens and businesses to conduct official business online, while data protection laws have helped to build public trust in digital services. Cybersecurity legislation, meanwhile, has established frameworks for responding to cyber threats and protecting critical infrastructure.

Open access policies for government networks and subsea cables have further encouraged competition among service providers, driving down costs and expanding connectivity to underserved areas. By opening up government infrastructure to private sector use, these policies have created new opportunities for innovation and investment. The resulting increase in competition has benefited consumers, who now enjoy more affordable and reliable internet services.

Collaboration has been at the heart of these successes. Ministries of ICT, education, and finance have worked closely together to align projects with broader development goals. This whole-of-government approach has ensured that digital initiatives are not pursued in isolation, but as part of a coherent strategy for national development. Private sector partners have also played a vital role, providing technical expertise, investment, and innovative solutions. In many cases, public-private partnerships have enabled governments to stretch limited resources further and to benefit from the agility and creativity of the private sector.

Despite these achievements, the journey has not been without its challenges. Budgetary constraints have been a persistent obstacle. The cost of deploying and maintaining digital infrastructure is significant, and fluctuations in funding have led to delays in project approval and implementation. In some cases, projects have had to be scaled back or reprioritized in response to budget shortfalls. The reliance on donor funding, while helpful, has also introduced complexities, as governments must balance local needs with donor priorities and reporting requirements.

Resistance to change has been another major hurdle. The introduction of new technologies and processes often disrupts established routines and requires public sector employees, educators, and even citizens to acquire new skills. In the education sector, for example, some teachers were initially hesitant to adopt e-learning tools, fearing that they would be unable to keep pace with technological change or that their roles would be diminished. Similarly, in the public sector, concerns about job security and increased workloads have sometimes slowed the adoption of digital systems. Overcoming this resistance has required sustained efforts in capacity building, communication, and change management.

Infrastructure gaps remain, particularly in the education sector. While many schools now have access to high-speed internet, the lack of adequate computer labs, devices, and technical support has limited the reach and impact of ICT initiatives. In some cases, connectivity has outpaced the availability of digital content and teacher training, resulting in underutilization of new platforms. Addressing these gaps requires ongoing investment, as well as partnerships with the private sector and civil society to mobilize additional resources.

Legal and regulatory gaps also persist. The rapid pace of technological change means that laws and policies are often playing catch-up. New challenges, such as the regulation of artificial intelligence, the protection of digital rights, and the management of cross-border data flows, require constant vigilance and adaptation. In some cases, the lack of up-to-date legislation has created uncertainty for businesses and consumers, potentially deterring investment and innovation.

Despite these difficulties, several key lessons emerge from the Eastern Caribbean experience. Strategic leadership is essential. High-level commitment from political leaders and senior officials has been critical for overcoming inertia, aligning efforts across government, and mobilizing resources. In both Grenada and St. Vincent and the Grenadines, the personal involvement of prime ministers, ministers of ICT, and other senior leaders has sent a clear signal that digital transformation is a national priority.

Comprehensive policy and regulatory frameworks provide the structure needed for effective ICT integration. These frameworks not only set the vision and objectives for digital transformation but also establish the governance, legal, and operational foundations necessary for implementation. They create a level playing field for all stakeholders, ensure accountability, and provide mechanisms for monitoring and evaluation. The experience of Grenada and St. Vincent and the Grenadines demonstrates that robust frameworks are not a luxury, but a necessity for navigating the complexities of digital transformation.

Inclusive and sustained collaboration among public sector partners, private sector actors, and end-users enhances buy-in and project outcomes. When stakeholders are involved from the outset, they are more likely to support and champion digital initiatives. Collaboration also enables the pooling of resources, the sharing of expertise, and the identification of innovative solutions to complex challenges. The establishment of steering committees, technical working groups, and public-private partnerships has been instrumental in building trust and ensuring that projects reflect the needs and aspirations of all stakeholders.

Flexibility and adaptability in planning and implementation are also crucial. The digital landscape is constantly evolving, and governments must be prepared to respond to changing circumstances and emerging challenges. This requires a willingness to experiment, to learn from experience, and to adjust strategies as needed. In both countries, pilot projects, phased implementation, and regular reviews have enabled governments to test new approaches, scale successful initiatives, and course-correct when necessary.

The broader implications of these findings are significant. By navigating government networks and policies effectively, Caribbean countries can harness the transformative potential of ICT to drive economic growth, improve public sector efficiency, and enhance the quality of life for their citizens. The experiences of Grenada and St. Vincent and the Grenadines demonstrate that, even in resource-constrained settings, policy-driven ICT transformation is possible when there is strategic leadership, comprehensive frameworks, and a commitment to collaboration. These lessons are not only relevant for other countries in the Caribbean but also for small states and developing countries around the world that are seeking to leverage digital technologies for sustainable development.

In summary, the case of Grenada and St. Vincent and the Grenadines offers a powerful testament to the importance of policy-driven ICT transformation. It shows that with vision, planning, and partnership, even the most daunting challenges can be overcome. As digital technologies continue to reshape economies and societies, the experiences of these Eastern Caribbean countries provide a roadmap for others to follow—a roadmap grounded in leadership, collaboration, and an unwavering commitment to progress.

Conclusion

The journey of ICT integration in the Eastern Caribbean, as explored throughout this chapter, reveals a landscape marked by both remarkable progress and persistent complexity. The role of government is central in this narrative, serving as both architect and steward of the digital transformation process. Governments in the region have been called upon to set the vision, build the foundations, and orchestrate the myriad actors required to bring about meaningful change. Yet, as the experiences of countries like Grenada and St. Vincent and the Grenadines have shown, this role is not without its challenges. The dual capacity of governments to enable or hinder digital transformation is a recurring theme, one that underscores the importance of thoughtful policy, effective regulation, and collaborative practice.

At the heart of successful ICT integration lies the development of robust policy frameworks. These frameworks are not mere statements of intent; they are living documents that chart the course for national digital agendas. They articulate clear goals for broadband expansion, e-government, digital literacy, and the integration of ICT into key sectors such as education and health. In the Eastern Caribbean, the most successful policy frameworks have been those that are both comprehensive and adaptable, capable of responding to the rapid evolution of technology and the shifting needs of society. They provide the scaffolding upon which digital transformation is built, ensuring that investments are strategic, resources are allocated efficiently, and initiatives are aligned with broader development objectives.

The regulatory environment is an equally critical component of ICT integration. Effective regulation fosters competition, protects consumers, and ensures that the benefits of digital transformation are widely shared. In the Eastern Caribbean, telecommunications liberalization has played a pivotal role in expanding access to high-speed internet and reducing costs for consumers. Data protection and privacy laws have begun to build public trust in digital services, while cybersecurity frameworks are increasingly recognized as essential for safeguarding critical infrastructure and sensitive information. However, the pace of technological change often outstrips the ability of legal and regulatory systems to keep up, creating gaps that can undermine progress. Governments must therefore remain vigilant, continuously reviewing and updating their regulatory frameworks to address emerging challenges and opportunities.

Collaboration among public sector partners is another cornerstone of effective ICT integration. Digital transformation initiatives are inherently cross-cutting, requiring coordination across ministries, agencies, and even levels of government. The establishment of steering committees, technical working groups, and cabinet-level bodies has proven effective in breaking down silos and fostering a culture of shared responsibility. Inclusive planning processes that engage all relevant stakeholders, including end-users, have enhanced buy-in and reduced resistance to change. Regular communication, capacity building, and the development of clear, documented procedures have further supported effective collaboration. The experiences of Grenada and St. Vincent and the Grenadines demonstrate that when public sector partners work together, they can overcome resource constraints, pool expertise, and drive innovation.

Yet, the path to digital transformation is fraught with obstacles. Budgetary constraints are a persistent reality for governments in the Eastern Caribbean. The costs associated with deploying and maintaining ICT infrastructure, training personnel, and developing digital content are significant, and fiscal space is often limited. External funding from international donors and development partners has been instrumental in bridging resource gaps, but reliance on such support introduces its own complexities. Governments must balance donor priorities with local needs, ensure sustainability beyond the life of funded projects, and navigate the reporting and accountability requirements that come with external assistance.

Resistance to change is another formidable challenge. The introduction of new technologies and processes disrupts established routines and requires individuals to acquire new skills and adapt to different ways of working. In the public sector, concerns about job security, increased workloads, and the perceived risks of digitalization can slow the adoption of new systems. In the education sector, teachers and administrators may be hesitant to embrace e-learning tools, fearing that they lack the necessary expertise or that technology will diminish the value of traditional pedagogy. Overcoming resistance requires sustained efforts in change management, including clear communication about the benefits of digital transformation, ongoing training and support, and the recognition of early adopters and champions.

Infrastructure gaps remain a significant barrier to the full realization of ICT's potential. While progress has been made in expanding broadband connectivity and deploying government-wide area networks, disparities persist, particularly in rural and underserved areas. The lack of adequate computer labs, devices, and technical support in schools limits the reach and impact of digital initiatives. Similarly, the uneven distribution of infrastructure across government agencies can create bottlenecks and hinder the integration of services. Addressing these gaps requires ongoing investment, innovative financing mechanisms, and partnerships with the private sector and civil society.

Legal and regulatory gaps are an ever-present risk in a rapidly changing digital landscape. The emergence of new technologies such as artificial intelligence, cloud computing, and the Internet of Things presents novel challenges for policymakers. Issues related to digital rights, cross-border data flows, and platform regulation require constant vigilance and adaptation. In some cases, the absence of up-to-date legislation has created uncertainty for businesses and consumers, potentially deterring investment and innovation. Governments must be proactive in updating their legal frameworks, drawing on regional and international best practices while tailoring solutions to local contexts.

Despite these challenges, the experiences of the Eastern Caribbean offer valuable lessons for other countries and regions embarking on their own digital transformation journeys. Strategic leadership is paramount. High-level commitment from political leaders and senior officials is essential for overcoming inertia, aligning efforts across government, and mobilizing resources. The personal involvement of prime ministers, ministers of ICT, and other senior leaders sends a clear signal that digital transformation is a national priority and creates the momentum needed to drive change.

Comprehensive policy and regulatory frameworks provide the structure needed for effective ICT integration. These frameworks set the vision and objectives for digital transformation, establish the legal and operational foundations for implementation, and create mechanisms for monitoring and evaluation. They ensure accountability, foster a level playing field for all stakeholders, and provide the flexibility needed to respond to changing circumstances. The experiences of Grenada and St. Vincent and the Grenadines demonstrate that robust frameworks are not a luxury but a necessity for navigating the complexities of digital transformation.

Inclusive and sustained collaboration among public sector partners, private sector actors, and end-users enhances buy-in and project outcomes. When stakeholders are involved from the outset, they are more likely to support and champion digital initiatives. Collaboration enables the pooling of resources, the sharing of expertise, and the identification of innovative solutions to complex challenges. The establishment of steering committees, technical working groups, and public-private partnerships has been instrumental in building trust and ensuring that projects reflect the needs and aspirations of all stakeholders.

Flexibility and adaptability in planning and implementation are also crucial. The digital landscape is constantly evolving, and governments must be prepared to respond to new developments and emerging challenges. This requires a willingness to experiment, to learn from experience, and to adjust strategies as needed. Pilot projects, phased implementation, and regular reviews have enabled governments in the Eastern Caribbean to test new approaches, scale successful initiatives, and course-correct when necessary.

The broader implications of these findings are significant. By navigating government networks and policies effectively, Caribbean countries can harness the transformative potential of ICT to drive economic growth, improve public sector efficiency, and enhance the quality of life for their citizens. The experiences of Grenada and St. Vincent and the Grenadines demonstrate that, even in resource-constrained settings, policy-driven ICT transformation is possible when there is strategic leadership, comprehensive frameworks, and a commitment to collaboration. These lessons are not only relevant for other countries in the Caribbean but also for small states and developing countries around the world that are seeking to leverage digital technologies for sustainable development.

The journey toward ICT integration is ongoing. As technology continues to evolve at a rapid pace, governments must remain agile, open to learning, and committed to continuous improvement. The integration of ICT is not a one-time event but a process that requires sustained effort, investment, and adaptation. Governments must cultivate a culture of innovation, empower public sector employees and citizens to embrace change, and foster partnerships that extend beyond the boundaries of government. By doing so, they can ensure that ICT serves as a powerful tool for national development and social progress.

In reflecting on the experiences of the Eastern Caribbean, it becomes clear that the integration of ICT is as much about people and processes as it is about technology. The success of digital transformation depends on the ability of governments to inspire, coordinate, and lead. It requires a vision that extends beyond the immediate challenges to encompass the broader possibilities of a digitally empowered society. It demands policies and regulations that are both rigorous and flexible, capable of safeguarding the public interest while enabling innovation. And it calls for a spirit of collaboration that unites stakeholders in pursuit of shared goals.

As other countries and regions look to the Eastern Caribbean for guidance, they would do well to remember that the path to digital transformation is neither linear nor easy. It is marked by setbacks as well as successes, by moments of doubt as well as breakthroughs. But with perseverance, strategic leadership, and a commitment to learning, governments can navigate the complexities of ICT integration and unlock new opportunities for their people. The lessons of the Eastern Caribbean are a testament to what is possible when vision, policy, and partnership come together in pursuit of a common purpose.

In conclusion, the role of government in ICT integration is both pivotal and complex. Governments can enable or hinder digital transformation through their policies, regulatory environments, and collaborative practices. The development of robust policy frameworks and supportive regulatory environments, combined with effective collaboration among public sector partners, is essential for realizing the full potential of ICT. The case of the Eastern Caribbean offers valuable insights into the opportunities and challenges of navigating government networks and policies, providing a roadmap for other countries and regions seeking to embark on their own digital transformation journeys. By learning from these experiences and remaining adaptable in the face of rapid technological change, governments can ensure that ICT integration serves as a powerful tool for national development and social progress. The future of digital transformation in the Caribbean and beyond will depend on the ability of governments to lead with vision, to govern with wisdom, and to collaborate with purpose.

Chapter 6

Overcoming Budgetary and Resource Challenges

Introduction

Navigating the path toward successful Information and Communication Technology (ICT) integration is fraught with considerable challenges, especially when it comes to budgetary and resource limitations. For project managers, policymakers, and stakeholders in the Eastern Caribbean, a region already contending with profound economic, geographic, and social constraints, these obstacles are even more acute. The combination of limited national budgets, exposure to unpredictable external shocks, and accession to technology-dependent global markets underscores the urgency of robust financial and resource strategies. Yet, what may appear as an impasse is, in reality, a crucible for innovation and adaptive leadership. It is within this context that strategic planning, dynamic management, judicious use of partnerships, and disciplined financial oversight become not just assets, but necessities for progress.

The ever-evolving landscape of ICT brings with it additional complexity. Rapid advancements in technology frequently outpace the adaptability of traditional funding models, placing further strain on national administrations and institutional leaders. Donor support, while critical for many large-scale projects, remains uncertain and often misaligned with local implementation capacities and long-term sustainability needs. Human resources, essential for both day-to-day operations and more ambitious transformation projects, must continually adapt to new roles, technologies, and expectations in environments where training budgets and up skilling opportunities may be modest. Success, therefore, is less about the absolute amount of funding or resources available, and more about the agility and precision with which these assets are deployed. Project leaders must become skilled architects, allocating, leveraging, and multiplying whatever financial, human, and infrastructural assets are at their disposal.

As government agencies, educational institutions, businesses, and civil society organizations across the Caribbean embrace digital transformation, the demand for transparent, accountable, and sustainable resource management rises sharply. The drive toward e-government, digital health, modern education, and smart business practices all exert pressure on established systems, demanding that both money and talent are not only spent wisely but tracked, measured, and justified with an eye toward both present impact and future scalability.

Within this framework, the chapter undertakes a comprehensive examination of the multifaceted challenges and the corresponding strategies for overcoming resource and budgetary constraints in ICT development. First, it explores the diversity of funding sources and allocation mechanisms available in the region. This includes a close look at public budgeting processes, the integration and limitations of internally generated revenues from ICT programs, the strategic use of development grants, and the often-complex world of public–private partnerships. Here, the emphasis falls on how these sources can be rigorously managed and continually optimized, not through static, annual routines, but via ongoing assessment and flexible redirection in response to changing needs.

The discussion then turns to the creative solutions that arise from necessity. Innovation is often catalyzed under constraint, and in the Eastern Caribbean, this has led to the emergence of lean implementation methodologies, the adoption of open-source and low-cost technologies, and inventive approaches to asset management and workforce development. Beyond technology, the section considers the mindsets and institutional cultures that allow for continuous adaptation, seeking out "quick wins" and leveraging everyday efficiencies in environments where every dollar counts.

Partnerships and donor relationships are given special attention as a critical lever for magnifying available resources and expertise. Effective partnership-building is much more than fundraising, it's about aligning interests with regional and international actors, unlocking complementary strengths, and ensuring local buy-in and ownership at every step. Through detailed examples and best practice guidance, the chapter shows how ongoing, transparent communication, shared monitoring frameworks, and a persistent focus on mutual benefit enable partnerships that endure and thrive, even as project priorities or external funding climates shift.

Finally, actionable guidance is provided on the nuts and bolts of budget management. Drawing from local case studies, field experience, and cross-regional comparisons, the chapter outlines processes for conducting needs assessments, instituting rigorous cost-benefit analyses, preparing transparent and realistic budgets, and implementing strong monitoring, documentation, and procurement practices. Emphasis is placed on continuous evaluation, the avoidance of common pitfalls, and the fostering of a culture of stewardship that values every resource, whether generated internally or sourced from external partners.

Interwoven throughout the discussion are lessons gleaned from the lived experiences of ICT project managers in the Eastern Caribbean, as well as insights from regional documentation and scholarship. These narratives provide a ground-level view of both the challenges faced and the innovative approaches developed in response. The result is a practical, evidence-based guide for practitioners determined to turn adversity into opportunity, building sustainable digital growth on foundations of resilience, creativity, and collaboration.

This chapter, ultimately, not only identifies the barriers to ICT advancement in resource-constrained contexts but offers a roadmap for leaders and practitioners to systematically overcome these challenges, harnessing proven strategies, cultivating partnerships, and ensuring that every resource, however limited has the opportunity to make a transformative difference.

Funding Models and Resource Allocation

Financial sustainability remains an essential cornerstone in the effective integration and ongoing support of ICT initiatives, especially within the unique landscape of the Eastern Caribbean. To achieve successful outcomes, project managers and policymakers must be adept at navigating the intricate web of available funding models, establish rigorous resource allocation strategies, and remain vigilant against the shifting tides of economic and political influence.

The Role of Government Budget Allocations

Government funding has historically underpinned many public ICT projects in the region, employing mechanisms such as line-item budgeting and annual appropriations to cover capital and operational costs. This traditional model offers certain advantages, including built-in accountability and alignment with national development strategies. However, the thesis emphasizes that such mechanisms are deeply susceptible to bureaucratic inertia: slow-moving approval processes, inflexible budget structures, and the ever-present risk of political transition can disrupt project implementation at critical junctures. Case study evidence from Grenada and St. Vincent and the Grenadines highlights that project managers often must contend with unexpectedly frozen or reallocated funds, forcing them to recalibrate timelines and, in some cases, reduce project scope or postpone key deliverables.

Furthermore, while a government's commitment can lend long-term credibility and institutional support to ICT integration, it also requires deliberate engagement with ministries, legislative bodies, and oversight committees. Embedding ICT projects in multi-year national development plans or within the mandates of dedicated ministries (such as a Ministry of ICT) has been shown to improve budgetary resilience and continuity, insulating projects somewhat from political shifts. However, the thesis notes that project managers must proactively engage stakeholders, perform rigorous needs assessments, and constantly advocate for the strategic importance of ICT initiatives in order to secure and sustain these government allocations.

International Aid and Development Grants: Opportunities and Limitations

International donors and multilateral financial institutions play an instrumental role in ICT development across the Caribbean. Agencies such as the World Bank, Inter-American Development Bank, UNDP, and regionally focused bodies like the OECS and CARICOM supply not only funding but also technical expertise, training programs, and project management support to drive large-scale ICT rollouts.

However, project managers report several recurring challenges in leveraging donor funds. The complex and often lengthy application processes, with substantial documentation and stringent reporting requirements, can burden local institutions with administrative overhead.

Disbursement timelines may not align with project milestones, causing cash flow bottlenecks or slowing procurement. An overreliance on external grants may also create a "dependency trap," where core operational and maintenance costs go unfunded once the original grant cycle ends. As found in the thematic analysis of Eastern Caribbean case studies, sustainability becomes precarious if internal mechanisms for securing revenue, such as user fees or government cost recovery are not concurrently developed.

To enhance long-term impact, the thesis recommends anchoring donor-funded projects within well-articulated national ICT strategies, fostering broad-based local buy-in, and structuring proposals to emphasize capacity-building elements that persist beyond the grant's lifespan. This approach also positions projects to attract follow-on funding and technical support from a more diversified donor base, improving overall program resilience.

Public-Private Partnerships (PPPs): Unlocking Collaborative Advantage

Public-private partnerships have emerged as a dynamic model for addressing funding and capacity gaps in Caribbean ICT initiatives. PPPs allow governments to tap into private sector capital and expertise, while also sharing the risks and rewards associated with infrastructure development and service delivery. According to the thesis, successful examples include broadband rollouts that leverage telecommunication providers' networks and operational experience, and the co-development of e-government platforms that draw on the innovation capacity of regional technology firms.

While PPPs bring distinct advantages, they are not without complexity. Negotiating clear governance arrangements, aligning incentives, and crafting performance-based contracts require governmental expertise and strong legal frameworks. The thesis stresses that transparent procurement processes, robust stakeholder engagement, and mechanisms for resolving disputes are all critical for sustainable PPPs. It is also vital that public partners retain sufficient strategic and operational control to safeguard national interests, ensure equitable access, and oversee compliance with broader policy goals.

Internally Generated Revenue (IGR): Building Toward Sustainability

Some governments and agencies have proactively sought to create self-sustaining funding streams to support ongoing ICT operations and upgrades. Internally generated revenue (IGR) is typically realized through service fees, licensing charges, sector-specific levies, or value-added offerings enabled by the digital transformation of government services.

When implemented thoughtfully, these mechanisms can create a positive feedback loop for sustainability. For instance, revenue from processing electronic licenses, registrations, or business permits can be earmarked to maintain and upgrade ICT systems, gradually reducing dependency on external funding. The thesis, drawing on

that digital transformation remains achievable even amidst resource constraints, ultimately delivering lasting benefits to governments, businesses, and citizens across the region.

Strategic Approaches to Resource Allocation in ICT Project Management

Efficient and effective deployment of resources is central to the success of ICT initiatives in the Eastern Caribbean and similar developing contexts. The process goes beyond simply securing funds; it involves making deliberate, evidence-based decisions to ensure those resources are used where they can yield the most meaningful and sustainable impacts. A review of findings and lived experiences from regional ICT project managers reveals several nuanced, context-specific strategies for maximizing outcomes with limited resources.

Project Prioritization: Aligning with Strategic Objectives

The reality of constrained budgets and competing needs means not all projects can progress simultaneously or at the same level of intensity. In practice, project managers, especially within government and public sector institutions, must perform rigorous needs assessments to distinguish between "must-have" and "nice-to-have" projects. Senior leaders are often tasked with convening steering committees or cross-ministerial working groups to ensure project selection aligns with overarching strategies for national development, digital transformation, or public sector reform.

This focus on mission-critical projects ensures that resources are not diluted across too many low-impact initiatives. Participants in the thesis study emphasized that integrating such prioritization into organizational culture lifts barriers to buy-in, increases accountability, and lays a foundation for more successful ICT integration at scale.

Phased Rollouts: Building in Flexibility and Agility

One of the core lessons from case studies on ICT initiatives in the Eastern Caribbean is that large, monolithic projects are inherently challenging to manage and sustain. These extensive undertakings often suffer from a lack of flexibility, exposing them to a variety of external and internal risks. Notably, shifts in user requirements or rapid technological advancements can render such projects obsolete before they even reach completion. Additionally, the sizeable nature of these projects makes them particularly vulnerable to funding interruptions; if a sudden shortfall occurs, the entire initiative may be placed in jeopardy rather than just a small part of it.

To address these challenges, project managers have increasingly favored breaking complex ICT projects into distinct, manageable phases, a process commonly referred to as phased implementation. This strategy unlocks several significant advantages. Firstly, the adoption of a phasing approach introduces a system of "gated progression," where each stage of the project serves as a critical checkpoint. At the end of every phase, project teams and stakeholders have the opportunity to conduct thorough evaluations of what has been accomplished, assess ongoing challenges, and make informed decisions about adjusting objectives or methodologies before moving forward. These checkpoints create natural moments for reflection and recalibration, reducing the risk of unnoticed errors compounding over time.

Furthermore, phasing a project enhances overall risk management. When the bulk of financial and organizational resources are invested in incremental steps rather than all at once, organizations can contain and minimize potential losses. If a particular aspect of the project is not working as intended in the early stages or if unforeseen barriers arise, only a limited segment of the project is affected. This "fail small" approach makes it possible for managers to quickly learn from setbacks, implement corrective actions, and protect the broader endeavor from significant financial or reputational harm.

Another benefit of the phased implementation method is the ability to secure incremental benefits early in the project lifecycle. Rather than requiring stakeholders to wait for the completion of a vast, all-encompassing system, the initial phases can focus on delivering immediate, high-impact results. Improvements in service delivery, establishment of critical data-sharing platforms, or the rollout of core functionalities can be achieved early, helping to build stakeholder confidence and momentum for future phases. These early successes also provide tangible evidence of progress, which can be leveraged to sustain support from funders, policymakers, and end-users throughout subsequent stages.

Concrete examples of this approach can be seen in the implementation of government-wide area networks and digital records systems across Grenada and St. Vincent and the Grenadines. Project leaders in these countries deliberately divided their initiatives into several clearly defined components. Each component came with specific deliverables, measurable evaluation criteria, and explicit decision points often referred to as go/no-go gates. This structure made it easier to monitor progress, allocate resources efficiently, and halt or adapt workstreams if changing conditions warranted a different course. As a result, not only were these projects more resilient to interruptions and unexpected challenges, but they also laid down the essential groundwork for scaling and future upgrades in a highly dynamic technological environment.

Zero-Based Budgeting: Justifying Every Dollar

Zero-based budgeting (ZBB) has become an increasingly important tool in the pursuit of fiscal discipline, particularly within ICT environments where entrenched spending habits and legacy budget lines may continue unchecked simply out of routine. Unlike traditional budgeting approaches, which often carry over prior expenditures without critical assessment, ZBB requires each department and project to start from a figurative "ground zero" in every new budget cycle. Under this approach, every proposed expenditure, no matter how established or seemingly essential—must be justified in direct relation to current operational priorities and clearly documented needs.

The adoption of zero-based budgeting serves several vital purposes in ICT project management. First, it shines a spotlight on outdated, redundant, or poorly aligned expenditures that may have lingered for years. Such expenditures can include licenses for underutilized software, maintenance contracts for obsolete hardware, or training initiatives no longer aligned with organizational strategy. By forcing a line-by-line analysis, ZBB helps organizations confront uncomfortable questions about spending that may have escaped scrutiny during routine budget renewals.

Another major advantage of ZBB is that it initiates structured discussions about trade-offs and opportunity costs. Since no expense is guaranteed, managers are obligated to articulate why a particular allocation is necessary and what would be foregone if that expense were excluded. These conversations foster a habit of weighing every investment against alternatives, making it easier to channel limited resources toward high-impact activities rather than spreading funds thinly across less critical areas.

Zero-based budgeting also fosters a culture of continuous improvement and strategic reflection, in stark contrast to the complacency that can set in when budgets follow established patterns without questioning their ongoing relevance. Departments are encouraged to question their assumptions, explore efficiencies, and seek innovative solutions rather than simply repeating previous spending directions. In the context of ICT rollouts, such as new software deployments, hardware upgrades, or capacity-building programs; this often leads to the identification of hidden costs or unnecessary redundancies and uncovers opportunities for greater operational efficiency.

According to ICT leaders interviewed in the thesis, introducing ZBB was instrumental in exposing gaps and inefficiencies that might have otherwise remained invisible. The process not only highlighted costs that could be trimmed or reallocated but also opened up new possibilities for resource optimization during major transitions such as system upgrades or staff development initiatives. By embedding zero-based budgeting into organizational routines, ICT teams and financial managers developed a shared sense of ownership and accountability around resource use, helping to ensure that each dollar is deployed where it can achieve the greatest value and most substantial results.

Performance-Based Funding: Linking Money to Results

In the context of ICT project management, a growing number of organizations in the Eastern Caribbean are transitioning away from traditional models of resource allocation where funding was often distributed based on historical precedents or projected needs to the more dynamic and results-oriented approach of performance-based funding. This shift is particularly evident in projects that rely on donor support, where accountability, measurable progress, and the demonstration of impact are critical to unlocking successive rounds of financial support.

Performance-based funding models are structured around the achievement of clearly defined milestones or outcomes.

Rather than receiving full funding upfront, project teams are provided with tranches of financial support only when they have met specific targets agreed upon in advance. For example, one common milestone is the attainment of key digital service delivery benchmarks. This could involve the launch of a new e-government platform, the integration of digital record systems across ministries, or achieving a certain percentage of public adoption of a new online service. By tying funding to the realization of these benchmarks, project managers and teams are motivated to focus their resources and efforts on the most impactful activities and to drive timely, measurable progress.

Another critical component of performance-based models is the implementation of training programs and the achievement of certification or competency targets among staff. Instead of simply allocating funds for training with no follow-up, these models require project teams to demonstrate that their personnel have successfully completed prescribed courses, earned professional certifications, or otherwise upgraded their skills to meet evolving project demands. This ensures that capacity-building is not only funded but is actually achieved by helping to create a more skilled, adaptable workforce ready to maintain and expand digital services.

Demonstrable improvements form another cornerstone of this funding approach. Funders may stipulate that a project must show quantifiable enhancements in areas such as data availability, system uptime, or user engagement with newly deployed platforms before additional resources are released. For instance, a government data integration project may be required to increase the amount and reliability of key datasets accessible to other agencies, or a public service portal might need to double its monthly user base. Regular, transparent reporting and the use of objective key performance indicators (KPIs) are essential tools in verifying progress and justifying further investment.

The move to performance-based funding not only incentivizes IT project teams to operate more efficiently and to prioritize activities with the highest potential for impact, but it also helps to instill a culture of results and accountability throughout the organization. Externally, such an approach is highly attractive to donors and development partners, who are increasingly under pressure to demonstrate the value and effectiveness of their contributions. By ensuring that funding decisions are grounded in clear evidence of progress, performance-based models help to build confidence among funders, foster sustainable relationships, and increase the prospects for ongoing support of ICT integration initiatives.

Importantly, the adoption of such models requires robust planning, transparent communication with all stakeholders, and the establishment of reliable systems for monitoring and evaluation. Project managers must work closely with donors and partners to agree on realistic, meaningful milestones and to ensure that data collection and reporting mechanisms are in place. As these practices become more widespread, they contribute to a more professionalized, outcomes-driven approach to ICT development one that maximizes the impact of every donor dollar and propels the digital transformation agendas of resource-constrained regions.

Capacity Building and Cross-Functional Deployment

The limited pool of ICT professionals in the region makes multi-skilling essential. Investments in capacity building through targeted staff training, peer knowledge sharing, and formal mentorship programs enable organizations to cover skills gaps without continually hiring external consultants. Cross-functional deployment, such as assigning technical staff to support both infrastructural upgrades and end-user training, cultivates organizational agility and responsiveness.

The thesis reinforces that building internal ICT talent pipelines is not only cost-effective but also critical to sustaining and scaling digital transformation over the long term.

Resource Pooling and Centralized Services

The practice of resource pooling and centralizing IT services has become an increasingly vital strategy for maximizing economies of scale, especially among regional governments with limited budgets. Rather than allowing each agency or department to independently manage their own procurement, system maintenance, and helpdesk operations, the move toward centralized services enables organizations to consolidate resources, streamline processes, and ultimately achieve much greater cost efficiency.

Centralized procurement stands out as a critical component of this strategy. By aggregating purchasing needs across multiple ministries or even entire countries, governments and public sector organizations can harness their collective buying power to negotiate more favorable contracts with vendors. This approach typically results in significant discounts on software licenses, hardware acquisitions, and IT infrastructure, since suppliers are often willing to offer better pricing and terms to larger purchasing groups. Moreover, bulk purchasing agreements reduce administrative overhead, eliminate duplicative efforts, and minimize the risk of misaligned or incompatible technology investments across agencies.

In addition to procurement, the establishment of regional-level data centers and e-government platforms represents a fundamental leap forward in service centralization. These shared infrastructures serve multiple departments or government entities, providing secure, scalable, and reliable digital services that might otherwise be unattainable for smaller administrations acting alone. For example, a regional data center can host cloud-based services, shared databases, and interoperable applications used by a range of public agencies, as well as facilitate disaster recovery and business continuity for critical government operations. The centralization of such technical resources not only lowers the investment needed from individual departments but also ensures a consistent level of security, compliance, and performance across the board.

Another important aspect of resource pooling involves collaborative training and certification programs. By organizing joint professional development initiatives, governments and partner organizations can standardize skillsets across the workforce, reduce the per-participant cost of specialized training providers, and create a culture of knowledge sharing. These programs also help to foster links between agencies, enabling better communication and collaboration which prove invaluable during cross-departmental IT projects or when responding to region-wide challenges. With consistent training, staff members are equipped to handle a wider range of systems and technologies, further reducing the reliance on expensive external consultants.

Pooling both technical and financial resources mitigates the perennial risks associated with under-utilization and inconsistent standards of service delivery. Instead of some departments possessing excess capacity while others struggle with insufficient infrastructure or support, centralized services ensure an equitable distribution of resources and a higher baseline quality across jurisdictions. Through this approach, organizations benefit from increased resilience, the ability to scale resources quickly in response to emerging needs, and a stronger negotiating position when dealing with technology vendors or service providers.

In summary, resource pooling and centralized IT services not only generate immediate cost savings and operational efficiencies; they also lay the groundwork for more innovative, integrated, and sustainable digital transformation efforts throughout the public sector. These strategies are essential for governments seeking to maximize limited resources while enhancing the impact and reliability of their ICT initiatives.

Persistent Challenges in Resource Allocation

Even with advanced strategies and careful planning, a number of persistent challenges continue to undermine the efficiency and effectiveness of resource allocation in ICT projects, particularly within resource-limited settings such as the Eastern Caribbean. These obstacles are multi-dimensional and often interrelated, making them difficult to fully eliminate even in well-managed environments.

Budget Delays and Cash Flow Interruptions

A common and recurring issue revolves around the delayed release of funds, whether these are sourced from international donors or government ministries. In practice, project managers routinely face situations where anticipated budget disbursements do not materialize on schedule. The bureaucratic procedures governing both donor-funded and government-initiated projects often include multiple layers of approval and verification, leading to significant hold-ups. When funds are delayed, project timelines must be constantly adjusted, scope may need to be reduced, and in some cases, critical project components are postponed or canceled altogether. These interruptions can erode morale, weaken stakeholder confidence, and, in the worst scenarios, cause promising initiatives to stall indefinitely.

Currency and Market Volatility

Another substantial challenge is the unpredictability of currency exchange rates and broader market fluctuations. Many ICT projects in the Caribbean rely heavily on imported technologies such as software, hardware, or cloud-based services, exposing them to the risk of significant price changes. A sudden depreciation of the local currency or a spike in global prices for core technologies can create major discrepancies between planned budgets and actual expenditures. This uncertainty complicates financial planning, sometimes leading to either costly over-expenditure or, conversely, a scale-down of essential project elements to stay within fixed budget ceilings. Effective risk management strategies, such as hedging or maintaining contingency funds, are therefore critical but not always fully developed in public sector planning processes.

Underestimating the Total Cost of Ownership

Across numerous case studies, there is a well-documented tendency for project teams to focus primarily on initial investment costs while overlooking the longer-term, recurring expenses necessary to maintain, update, and secure ICT systems. Typical examples of these ongoing costs include user support services, periodic professional training and refreshers, scheduled hardware replacement cycles, cybersecurity upgrades, regular software licensing renewals, and compliance updates. Failing to budget accurately for the entire lifecycle of ICT assets results in systems quickly losing their effectiveness progressing

195

toward obsolescence far earlier than anticipated. This oversight often leads to a lack of funds for essential maintenance and support activities, which diminishes the return on initial investments and may even cause projects to fail entirely.

Cultural Resistance and Institutional Inertia

Finally, organizational culture itself can present a formidable barrier to efficient resource allocation. Even the most rigorously designed allocation models and change management frameworks may flounder if deeply rooted attitudes and practices within institutions are resistant to change. Entrenched prioritization of historical spending patterns, reluctance to intervene in departmental silos, or skepticism toward new methods of collaboration can all impede the effective redistribution of resources. This cultural inertia not only inhibits the pursuit of innovation and adaptive strategies but can foster passive resistance, resulting in resource inefficiencies and missed opportunities. Overcoming these barriers demands persistent leadership, internal advocacy, and ongoing dialogue to foster a culture that supports learning, flexibility, and cross-functional teamwork.

By recognizing and proactively addressing these persistent challenges, ICT project managers and policymakers can better safeguard the efficiency and sustainability of their initiatives, even in the face of limited resources and unpredictable external factors.

Recommendations for Enhanced Resource Allocation in ICT Projects

In order to maximize the effectiveness and sustainability of ICT investments across the Eastern Caribbean, it is essential to adopt a strategic and comprehensive approach to resource allocation. One fundamental recommendation is the establishment of multi-year, rolling budget frameworks. Unlike annual, static budgets, these frameworks provide a buffer against unpredictable funding disruptions and allow project managers to plan for phased investments over an extended period. By spreading financial commitments and anticipated expenditures across several years, organizations can implement projects incrementally, monitor progress, and make mid-course adjustments without facing major operational setbacks when short-term funding gaps arise. This approach fosters greater stability and the ability to pursue transformative projects that require sustained commitment, thus creating a more resilient basis for ICT development.

Alongside long-term budgeting, developing rigorous risk management plans is crucial. The volatility of currency exchange rates and other macroeconomic factors can significantly impact project costs, especially in nations highly dependent on imported technology. Formal risk management strategies must address these uncertainties by allocating contingency funds and regularly reviewing exposure to financial risks. This preparedness allows for rapid response to external shocks such as sudden devaluation or price hikes and ensures that essential project activities can continue even when adverse economic circumstances threaten initial budgets.

Mandating comprehensive lifecycle costing across all phases of project planning is another key recommendation. Often, the temptation in ICT investments is to focus primarily on the up-front procurement and deployment costs, neglecting the critical requirements of system updates, technical training, and ongoing maintenance. Embedding lifecycle costing into every funding application and budget line ensures that provisions are made for the continued functionality, security, and relevance of technologies well beyond the initial implementation. This forward-looking approach prevents systems from falling into obsolescence due to lack of resources for upgrades or user support, thereby protecting organizational investments and fostering long-term impact.

Regular interdepartmental reviews also play a vital role in enhancing resource efficiency. By systematically evaluating asset utilization, organizations can pinpoint underused equipment, duplicated purchases, or redundant processes. Such reviews promote the identification of opportunities for pooling resources like shared data centers, joint procurement of software licenses, or centralized technical support which in turn lowers overall costs and increases the quality and availability of ICT services. This culture of transparency and collaboration ensures that every dollar spent serves a collective strategic purpose, rather than being lost to inefficiency or isolation.

Finally, the establishment of clear, measurable key performance indicators (KPIs) is indispensable for effective resource allocation. Benchmarking performance against these KPIs facilitates ongoing alignment of resources with evolving organizational and sector-wide priorities. Regular analysis of performance data allows for agile adjustment of investments: scaling up successful initiatives, reallocating resources away from projects that are not meeting objectives, and identifying best practices that can be replicated. Through continuous performance monitoring, project managers ensure that allocation decisions are evidence-based and focused on achieving the highest possible return on investment, both in terms of service delivery and broader social impact.

When these practices are institutionally embedded and constantly refined in response to real-world lessons, they create the foundation for ICT programs that are truly sustainable, scalable, and socially transformative. For the Eastern Caribbean and similar regions, such a disciplined and dynamic approach to resource allocation is not just a technical exercise, but a critical lever for socioeconomic advancement, digital equity, and resilient public service delivery.

Creative Solutions for Doing More with Less

Resource constraints in the field of Information and Communication Technology (ICT) integration in the Eastern Caribbean and similar environments have, paradoxically, served as a powerful catalyst for innovation. The thematic analysis and case studies found in the thesis underscore that scarcity often compels organizations and project managers to break free from conventional resource-heavy paradigms and instead cultivate a spirit of adaptability, resilience, and creative problem-solving. This section expands upon the previously outlined approaches, weaving in local evidence and expert reflections to illustrate how necessity truly becomes the mother of invention in ICT project management.

One of the most transformative creative responses to resource scarcity is the adoption of agile project management. Insights from Eastern Caribbean ICT leaders reveal that actively employing iterative, feedback-driven processes enables project teams to launch functional deliverables rapidly and adjust to shifting requirements or constraints. By focusing on the concept of a minimum viable product (MVP), ICT managers are able to deliver critical services that generate immediate value, ensuring that limited investments target stakeholder priorities. Participants in the thesis interviews concluded that such adaptive methodologies not only reduce upfront risks but also allow projects to "fail small," learn quickly, and recalibrate approaches without sacrificing overall momentum or exhausting resources.

The thesis further documents the strategic embrace of open source and low-cost technologies as an engine of affordability and system flexibility. For Eastern Caribbean governments and institutions, leveraging freely available solutions such as Linux operating systems, open-source productivity suites, or cloud-hosted platforms like Moodle aligns perfectly with the constraints and demands of small island economies. These decisions are not made solely on cost grounds: the data show that customization, security, and user empowerment are all enhanced when proprietary barriers are removed. A key insight from the research was the deliberate structuring of IT policy to favor open standards and community-driven support networks, leading to software stacks that can be maintained and extended independent of any one vendor. The region's increasing reliance on cloud services also exemplifies doing more with less; cloud infrastructure enables flexible, scalable deployments that adapt to sudden shifts in demand without the need for heavy capital outlays or ongoing hardware maintenance.

Creative stewardship of physical assets emerged as another hallmark of self-reliant ICT management in the Eastern Caribbean. Several interviewed project managers described orchestrating structured programs for refurbishing and reassigning hardware switching older but serviceable laptops, desktops, and networking equipment from central offices to schools or smaller agencies thereby squeezing extended value from each procurement round. This cyclical approach to asset management not only stretches budgets but also fosters a culture of environmental sustainability and waste reduction, which is increasingly recognized as integral to modern ICT governance.

Within the realm of human resources, the thesis regularly highlights the pivotal role of cross-training and capacity building. In small or under-resourced organizations, having staff with multi-disciplinary expertise, combining, for example, network administration, cybersecurity, and end-user support which ensures operational continuity even as funding or personnel fluctuate. Structured mentorship arrangements, formal and informal knowledge transfer sessions, and the creation of digital playbooks for troubleshooting or onboarding new staff all contribute to an agile, skilled workforce that can collectively do more with less. These capacity-building exercises often minimize dependency on external consultants or outsourcing, leading to greater institutional resilience and a deeper sense of ownership among local teams.

The rise of remote and hybrid working arrangements has delivered further benefits. Empowering staff to work off-site, collaborate asynchronously, and draw on global best practices through virtual platforms has diminished the need for physical office expansion, reduced travel costs, and given organizations access to a broader and more diverse talent pool. The thesis draws particular attention to the engagement of diaspora experts and international volunteers, who are eager and often uniquely qualified to consult, mentor, or contribute remotely to local ICT development. These models bring in expertise that would otherwise be prohibitively expensive or unavailable, fueling sustained capacity growth at minimal incremental cost.

Another cornerstone of creative ICT strategy is direct community engagement. The research notes the significant impact of mobilizing local volunteers, ICT enthusiasts, and university students to work side by side with public agencies on targeted challenges. Initiatives such as hackathons, solution sprints, and joint research projects not only address pressing technical and operational pain points but also inspire community buy-in and foster pathways for workforce development. The participatory ethos documented in the thesis shows that when students and volunteers are actively included in systems design, deployment, and iterative troubleshooting, both parties stand to gain: agencies receive timely, tailored solutions, while participants acquire marketable skills, experience, and a personal stake in public innovation.

Efficiency gains are further amplified through thoughtful resource pooling and shared services. The thesis recounts how multi-agency partnerships, the centralization of support desks, and the deployment of regionally managed data centers have achieved substantial economies of scale. Projects that would have exceeded the reach of any one institution become feasible when investment risks, technical expertise, and maintenance responsibilities are distributed. Moreover, pooled procurement initiatives where multiple ministries or agencies band together to negotiate with vendors, significantly reduce per-unit costs and yield extended support agreements, stretching the value of each dollar spent.

A defining philosophy running throughout the thesis is the application of incrementalism and strategic adaptation. Rather than pursuing grand-scale digital transformation projects in a single leap, with all the attendant risks of misallocation and scope creep, Caribbean ICT leaders recommend piloting limited initiatives, testing assumptions in real-world conditions, and scaling up only proven models. This pragmatic approach provides real-time feedback, surfaces unforeseen challenges, and allows for the measured reallocation of resources as priorities shift or as previously funded projects conclude. Ongoing expenditure monitoring ensures that any residual funds or underutilized assets are redirected toward emergent needs, supporting institutional flexibility and sustained momentum.

Finally, the research makes it clear that sustainable innovation is as much about mindset as about mechanics. Constraints, rather than stifling ambition, are embraced as drivers of ingenuity. Through disciplined prioritization, the cultivation of versatile skill sets, the fostering of collaborative community networks, and the pursuit of flexible, open technology platforms, ICT managers in the Eastern Caribbean have repeatedly demonstrated their ability to deliver results that outstrip their material means. The lessons drawn from these experiences offer a replicable blueprint, grounded in real-world successes and setbacks, for other regions and sectors that must make progress under tight financial and human resource constraints.

Leveraging Partnerships and Donor Support: An In-depth Perspective

In the context of digital transformation within resource-limited regions, particularly the Eastern Caribbean, forging effective partnerships and securing donor support have emerged as linchpins for driving Information and Communication Technology (ICT) advancement. These collaborative strategies not only supplement scarce local resources but also bring in vital expertise, innovation, and credibility that are seldom achievable through local efforts alone. Drawing extensively on the findings and case narratives detailed in the thesis, this section delves into the approaches, dynamics, and essential practices characterizing successful partnership and donor engagement for ICT integration.

The Strategic Value of Collaboration

The criticality of cross-sectoral partnership comes to the fore in environments where public sector budgets for ICT are perpetually constrained and domestic technical capacity is stretched thin. As qualitative case studies with regional ICT leaders show, progress often hinges on the organization's ability to "extend their reach," both financially and technically, by scaling up collaboration:

In the context of ICT advancement in the Eastern Caribbean and similar developing regions, the cultivation of diverse partnerships is critical, not only as vehicles for financing, but as engines of knowledge transfer, innovation, and community engagement. These collaborative frameworks extend far beyond mere transactional relationships, providing the structure and momentum required for transformative ICT projects to take root and flourish.

Public-Private Partnerships (PPPs): Engines of Co-Creation and Capacity Building

Public-Private Partnerships (PPPs) have emerged as one of the most effective mechanisms for bridging resource gaps and accelerating ICT development in the region. Unlike traditional funding sources that focus solely on financial transfers, PPPs facilitate a dynamic process of co-creation, where government institutions offer regulatory access and strategic oversight, while private sector entities inject entrepreneurial agility, technical innovation, and project management expertise. Interviews with project managers across the Caribbean underscore the pivotal role PPPs have played in realizing major broadband infrastructure upgrades, implementing robust school connectivity schemes, and enabling complex e-government platforms tailored to local needs.

One of the most significant but often understated benefits of PPPs is their contribution to human capital development within the public sector. These partnerships are not limited to physical infrastructure projects; they serve as conduits for active knowledge transfer. Private sector specialists work directly with local teams, providing training, technical guidance, and operational insights. This direct, hands-on engagement builds local expertise and equips government staff with the skills needed for long-term management and innovation, creating a legacy that persists well beyond the duration of any individual project.

International Donor Agencies: Catalysts for Credibility and Systemic Change

International donor agencies are another central pillar in the realm of ICT advancement in the Caribbean. High-profile agencies such as the World Bank, the Inter-American Development Bank, and various bilateral donors provide more than just funding. Their multifaceted support often includes the deployment of structured project management frameworks, the implementation of standardized monitoring and evaluation protocols, and the provision of internationally trusted models for procurement and risk management. These elements establish strong operational foundations, reduce project risk, and allow for more transparent and accountable use of resources.

Perhaps most importantly, the involvement of respected international donors often functions as a "stamp of credibility" for local projects. Their endorsement signals to other funders and stakeholders, both governmental and private, that a particular initiative has been rigorously vetted and meets accepted benchmarks for quality and accountability. This reputation effect frequently spurs further investment and creates a favorable environment for additional governmental or private sector resources to flow into the local ICT ecosystem. International donors also act as connectors, linking regional actors to global networks of expertise, technologies, and best practices that would otherwise be difficult to access.

Academic and Research Institutions: Incubators of Innovation and Sustainable Capacity

Academic and research institutions—both local universities and international partners, play a transformative role in the development and sustainability of ICT projects. These institutions bridge the gap between theoretical knowledge and practical application through collaborative research initiatives, customized ICT curriculum development, and the integration of student interns or research assistants into ongoing technical projects. By embedding educational partners within core ICT activities, governments benefit not only from cutting-edge research but from the steady cultivation of a talent pipeline equipped to address future challenges.

The research underscores that several public agencies have proactively leveraged relationships with universities and technical schools to "seed" internal capacity. Such partnerships frequently facilitate knowledge transfer that is both sustainable and directly relevant to local contexts, as curricula and research projects are tailored to meet the specific technological and policy challenges at hand. Furthermore, these institutions often act as gateways to global technical expertise. By tapping into international networks for peer review, troubleshooting, and collaborative problem-solving, local agencies can greatly expand the range of solutions and innovations available to them, often at a fraction of the cost of external consultants or proprietary systems.

Civil Society and Professional Associations: Bridges between Policy and Community

Civil society organizations and professional associations serve as essential intermediaries in the ICT ecosystem. Their roles are diverse and impactful, ranging from organizing digital literacy campaigns and advocating for progressive policies, to mobilizing volunteers for technical deployments and community-based research. Chambers of commerce, sector-specific NGOs, and professional ICT societies are particularly effective at bridging governmental priorities with grassroots realities, ensuring that technological solutions remain relevant, culturally appropriate, and widely accessible.

These organizations function as trusted voices within communities, translating abstract policy directives into practical guidance and actionable opportunities for local stakeholders. They often spearhead digital inclusion initiatives, offer capacity building and training workshops, and create forums for public feedback on ICT policies or system rollouts. Their ability to convene stakeholders from across the public, private, and nonprofit sectors allows for the design and execution of projects that enjoy broad-based support and legitimacy.

Moreover, civil society groups frequently act as facilitators for donor engagement, demonstrating social value and community buy-in to prospective funders. By documenting outcomes and collecting real-world stories, these organizations make compelling cases for support, increasing the likelihood of sustained donor and government investment.

In sum, the impact of strategic partnerships in ICT development is profound and multidimensional. When governments, private enterprises, donors, academic institutions, and civil society work together, they create fertile ground not only for funding and infrastructure improvements, but for the continuous diffusion of knowledge, innovation, and best practices. The lessons gleaned from the Caribbean experience demonstrate that such alliances drive not just short-term project success, but the longer-term resilience and adaptability of digital transformation efforts across entire societies.

Foundations for Effective Partnerships

The research underscores that the impact of collaboration is determined less by the scale of investment and more by the quality of partnership structures and alignment of objectives.

Alignment of Mutual Interests:

Partnerships thrive only when the objectives of each partner are clear and broadly shared. The thesis notes that those projects which are "co-designed" through joint problem definition and solution design, rather than donor- or government-imposed priorities, are more likely to attract sustained commitment from all parties and to achieve impactful outcomes. This alignment must be revisited regularly and, when necessary, recalibrated through formal and informal consultation processes.

Structure and Governance:

Transparent, legally-grounded governance is a critical prerequisite for multi-stakeholder projects. Most successful collaborations operate with detailed memoranda of understanding (MOUs) or formal contractual agreements that specify roles, expectations, deliverables, mutual resource contributions, and clear dispute resolution mechanisms. These "architecture documents" minimize friction, build trust, and provide mechanisms for resolving inevitable disagreements and ambiguities.

Credibility and Track Record:

Demonstrating the ability to deliver, through a clear history of successful projects, adherence to compliance standards, and robust anti-corruption and fiduciary frameworks, is crucial, particularly when dealing with international funders and the private sector. Caribbean agencies that have secured repeat donor support consistently point to transparent processes, robust reporting, and regular impact evaluation as the foundations of their credibility and appeal to partners.

Regional and Pooled Approaches:

The thesis emphasizes the growing importance of regional collaboration. By participating in frameworks at the CARICOM or OECS level, agencies unlock access to collective funding arrangements and technical platforms otherwise unavailable to single countries or institutions. Such pooled arrangements create economies of scale and present unified bargaining positions with vendors and funders, as was evident in several cross-island broadband and data center initiatives.

Community and Stakeholder Buy-in:

Engagement with local communities and end-users is cited as both a pathway to relevance and a persuasive factor in donor and partner negotiations. When project beneficiaries are involved in needs assessments, pilot implementations, and feedback cycles, project proposals gain legitimacy, and implementation risks are substantially reduced.

Donor Relationship Management: Best Practices

Beyond initial funding, relationships with donors require ongoing, deliberate management. Key insights from the thesis include:

In small countries, particularly within the Eastern Caribbean, the influx of multiple donor-funded ICT projects can inadvertently result in fragmented efforts. This fragmentation often manifests as duplication of activities, inconsistent requirements, or competition for the same limited pool of local staff and vendor resources. To address these inefficiencies, the thesis highlights the importance of establishing structured coordination mechanisms among stakeholders. Regular coordination forums, such as scheduled meetings, donor working groups, and the use of shared reporting or knowledge management tools play a vital role in facilitating open dialogue, aligning objectives, and synchronizing timelines. By bringing all relevant donors, government representatives, and implementing partners to the same table, these forums help to map current and upcoming activities, ensure accountability, and identify synergy opportunities. The collaborative approach not only mitigates overlapping mandates but also maximizes the collective impact of donor investments across the sector.

Embedding each project within broader, recognized ICT strategies is another cornerstone for success. Projects that are firmly rooted in comprehensive national or regional strategies are far more likely to attract and retain donor interest and funding. Donors generally prefer their contributions to serve as integrated building blocks for long-term transformational change, not as isolated interventions. As such, the existence of transparent, up-to-date strategic policy documents and action plans demonstrates government commitment and strategic vision. These frameworks clarify priorities, set measurable targets, and provide a sound basis for both proposal development and performance monitoring. This strategic anchoring reassures donors that their investments will contribute to systemic improvements and increases the likelihood of sustained support throughout a project's lifecycle.

Transparency and robust impact measurement are critical components in the maintenance and growth of donor relationships. As projects advance beyond initial funding cycles, the focus naturally shifts toward ensuring that resources are being used effectively and are generating tangible, quantifiable results. The thesis documents regional best practices in financial stewardship, such as the implementation of trusted financial management software, adherence to routine and rigorous reporting cycles, and engagement of third-party audits. These measures of openness not only satisfy donor compliance requirements but also build trust and confidence, which are essential for unlocking additional funding, scaling up successful initiatives, or securing project renewals. Transparent processes and credible impact data position project managers as reliable partners and make a compelling case for continued or expanded collaboration.

Finally, the most durable and productive donor relationships are those that extend beyond individual funding rounds or singular projects. Building enduring partnerships necessitates an active, deliberate approach to relationship management. This includes fostering an environment of mutual trust and respect, maintaining open, two-way communication about both achievements and challenges, and being transparent about evolving needs or shifting circumstances. Organizations that regularly engage donors in dialogue, solicit feedback, and share learning outcomes stand out as trustworthy and adaptable partners. Over time, these ongoing engagements help donors become more deeply invested in the broader vision and mission of the organization. As a result, donors are often more willing to provide increased flexibility, support innovation, and adapt to changing project or contextual realities, thereby contributing to more sustainable and impactful ICT development outcomes.

Challenges and Mitigation Strategies

Despite these success factors, recurring obstacles were identified:

A key challenge that often emerges in multi-stakeholder ICT development initiatives particularly those in resource-limited environments is the problem of fragmentation. When multiple projects are launched in parallel, supported by a diverse array of donors, agencies, and partner organizations, the absence of centralized coordination can result in efforts working at cross-purposes. This scenario may lead to a duplication of activities, competition for the same limited local resources, and even contradictory goals or approaches among different stakeholders. Such a lack of coherence not only diminishes the efficiency and effectiveness of resource use but also fosters the phenomenon commonly referred to as "pilotitis." In this context, organizations repeatedly implement pilot projects, gathering short-term data or demonstrating potential solutions that rarely scale up to broader, systemic change. Over time, this cycle drains organizational energy and undermines the potential for sustainable, far-reaching impact.

Another significant barrier is the issue of capacity constraints. Managing partnerships, especially those involving donors and international agencies, is inherently resource-intensive. The administrative requirements including day-to-day coordination, reporting, compliance with various funding regulations, and consistent communication with multiple stakeholders can easily surpass the capacity of understaffed teams. Regional experience across the Caribbean underscores the necessity for organizations to invest purposefully in dedicated project management roles. Professional project managers or donor relationship officers bring specialized expertise, ensure that projects remain on track, and serve as vital bridges between the organizations, its partners, and the communities served. Their presence not only streamlines engagement but also builds trust by upholding high standards of accountability and responsiveness.

Equally critical is the question of sustainability, which is often compromised when projects are propelled chiefly by donor agendas rather than being locally owned and embedded. When initiatives are designed and implemented according to external priorities, with minimal engagement from local stakeholders or beneficiaries, their long-term relevance and viability may be limited. Once the initial influx of donor funding concludes, organizations may struggle to maintain or expand the project, leading to a gradual erosion of benefits and, ultimately, project abandonment. To counter this, it is essential that capacity-building initiatives and concrete sustainability strategies are woven into every partnership from the outset. This involves not only training local staff and building organizational expertise but also establishing ongoing funding mechanisms, maintenance plans, and strong community ownership. Enduring success hinges on partnerships that are both responsive to donor requirements and firmly grounded in the local context, ensuring that achievements are preserved and built upon even after donor involvement decreases or ends.

The experience of ICT project leaders in the Eastern Caribbean illuminates that partnership far more than financial capital alone is the keystone for overcoming budgetary limits. Success emanates from collaborative architectures that carefully align organizational and partner priorities, build transparent and accountable governance scaffolding, and invest unwaveringly in both community and donor relationships. As Caribbean institutions move deeper into digital transformation, their ability to skillfully leverage partnerships and donor networks will continue to define the pace and quality of regional ICT integration.

Practical Tips for Budget Management: In-Depth Guidance

The Critical Foundation of Needs Assessment

Effective budget management in ICT projects, especially across the Eastern Caribbean, begins with a comprehensive and participatory needs assessment. The thesis emphasizes that project leaders must not only inventory existing assets, infrastructure, and IT skillsets, but also actively involve end-users and frontline staff in early consultations. This inclusivity uncovers hidden requirements and future costs that are often overlooked when planning is limited to management or technical experts alone. Multiple case studies in Grenada and St. Vincent and the Grenadines revealed that projects which failed to surface user-driven needs at the start encountered significant scope creep, costly mid-course corrections, or even adoption failures once solutions were deployed.

Engaging stakeholders at all levels through structured surveys, workshops, and feedback sessions adds rigor to gap analyses and helps clarify which investments are truly critical versus discretionary. The research underscores that, in resource-limited environments, every unanticipated requirement represents a potential risk to both financial and operational success.

Rigorous Cost–Benefit Prioritization for Resource Allocation

Once needs are mapped, the thesis highlights the importance of prioritizing projects based on a clear assessment of return on investment (ROI), impact, and risk. Interviewed project managers described using objective frameworks and scoring matrices to rank initiatives according to their alignment with strategic goals, cost-effectiveness, and capacity for sustainable impact.

This practice is coupled with explicit risk-adjusted planning: organizations are urged to allocate contingency funds for the unexpected, recognizing that both technical and market environments can shift rapidly. This approach is particularly vital in developing contexts, where exchange-rate volatility, vendor changes, or political shifts can quickly alter the feasibility or cost of ICT initiatives.

Realistic and Transparent Budgeting Practices

The thesis stresses that the budgeting process must be rooted in up-to-date market intelligence and historical spending data. This realism helps avoid the chronic underestimation of costs that derails so many projects. Budgets should be broken down into detailed categories covering hardware, software, services, training, travel, and maintenance which supports precise tracking and flagging of variances. The research found that such granularity not only aids in day-to-day financial control but also provides insights for continuous improvement in future budgeting cycles.

Scenario planning is another best practice detailed in the case studies. By preparing for best-case, expected, and worst-case financial environments, organizations enable themselves to adapt quickly if funding levels change, whether due to external donor decisions or internal reallocations. The use of phased funding releasing only the resources needed for initial project stages and then scaling up as results and new resource streams emerge was credited by several managers with saving projects that otherwise would have faced insurmountable cash-flow challenges.

Expenditure Monitoring and Approval Controls

Operational discipline during budget execution is essential. The thesis describes various methods used by Caribbean ICT managers to maintain accurate, up-to-date records on all expenditures. Whether through widely available accounting software or robust spreadsheet systems, daily tracking is advised to enable early detection of overruns or under-utilization.

Structured approval hierarchies are used to safeguard integrity and accountability. Routine expenses have clearly defined thresholds for sign-off, while exceptional or large expenditures require escalation to higher-level managers or committees. Such controls were especially valued in donor-funded projects, where compliance with international fiduciary standards is not only good practice but often a precondition for further support.

Procurement and Vendor Management for Maximum Value

Achieving value for money in public ICT procurement is a recurring focus in the thesis. All participating managers favored fully transparent, competitive tendering processes that encourage price discovery, discourage favoritism, and improve the quality of goods and services received. The regular evaluation and renegotiation of vendor contracts taking account of performance, bundled services, and discounts were cited as both a cost-saving measure and a way to hold suppliers accountable for their commitments.

Pooling procurement across agencies or departments emerged as a simple yet effective measure for delivering discounts through economies of scale. Several participants shared examples where joint purchasing of software licenses, network equipment, or consulting services reduced individual project costs while raising the overall standard of support.

Comprehensive service agreements, which consolidate multiple needs (e.g., hardware, maintenance, and training) under a single contract, were also highlighted as a best practice. This approach streamlines contract management, eases troubleshooting, and can limit vendor "lock-in" a common pitfall in fragmented or piecemeal procurement environments.

Strategic Cost Containment beyond Simple Cuts

The thesis strongly advocates for strategic cost-containment, shifting the focus from mere expenditure reductions to maximizing the impact of every dollar spent. Some of the most cited practices include consolidating licensing arrangements, negotiating broad "all-in-one" service contracts, and prioritizing modular, upgradeable solutions that minimize future refresh expenses. Organizations that proactively design their infrastructure for flexibility and easy upgrades minimize both initial and life-cycle costs.

The research warns against reactive, across-the-board cuts, urging instead that savings be sought through smarter investment and process redesign: for example, replacing bespoke, high-maintenance systems with open-source options, or leveraging cloud solutions to limit capital expenditures and align costs with actual usage patterns.

Continuous Evaluation and Adaptive Management

Financial stewardship does not end with the initial budget cycle. The thesis recommends instituting regular variance analysis comparing actual versus budgeted expenditures at frequent intervals to surface deviations early and support prompt course correction. At the close of each project or phase, leaders should conduct structured post-implementation reviews, documenting both successes and shortfalls in detail.

These reviews provide valuable inputs into organizational learning cycles, enabling teams to refine their budgeting assumptions, processes, and controls for future projects. The iterative feedback loop is particularly valuable in dynamic digital environments, where technological change often outpaces traditional budgeting processes.

Proactive Strategies to Avoid Common Pitfalls

Through interviews and case document analysis, the thesis identifies several persistent risks to effective budget management and prescribes actionable mitigation tactics:

A recurring challenge in ICT project management lies in the tendency to underestimate the total cost of ownership. Many organizations focus heavily on securing the initial capital required for projects such as the purchase of hardware and software while failing to account for the recurring costs that inevitably arise over the project lifecycle. Expenses for ongoing maintenance, periodic training for staff, and essential system upgrades are vital for keeping technology relevant and operational. Without proactively allocating funds for these recurrent needs, systems quickly become outdated, inefficient, or prone to failure. Therefore, effective budgeting must extend beyond the initial outlay, reflecting a complete view that ensures long-term sustainability and support for the deployed ICT infrastructure.

Another substantial risk is the delayed release of project funding, particularly where disbursements are tied to donor timelines or complex public sector procedures. These delays can stall project progress, erode team morale, and even threaten the project's viability altogether. To mitigate such impacts, it is advisable for managers to develop conservative, realistic implementation schedules that allow for inevitable funding gaps. Alongside this, maintaining a portfolio of low-cost, quick-win activities that can be executed during periods of financial uncertainty keeps project momentum alive. These tactical initiatives can help organizations make the best use of available resources while awaiting larger funding tranches.

Over-reliance on a single donor or funding stream is another pitfall that can expose projects to significant vulnerability. Should a donor alter its priorities, withdraw support, or experience its own financial constraints, a project may face sudden and severe resource shortages. Developing a diversified funding base, which includes cultivating relationships with multiple donors and exploring options for generating internal revenues such as through service fees or local partnerships helps cushion the impact of donor cycles or abrupt changes in external support. This approach builds resilience and promotes the long-term sustainability of ICT initiatives.

Weak accountability structures often undermine the effectiveness and credibility of ICT projects. Without strong documentation practices, regular financial and operational reporting, and strict expenditure approval frameworks, transparency is compromised and opportunities for mismanagement or misuse of funds increase. Especially in donor-funded initiatives, demonstrating rigorous compliance and transparent controls is critical for maintaining funder trust and project legitimacy. Establishing these processes from the outset helps to ensure all activities are conducted responsibly and in line with best practices.

One often-overlooked aspect of ICT planning is the need for ongoing technology refreshment. The rapid pace of technological change can render systems obsolete within a few years if proactive upgrade strategies are not implemented. Organizations must plan for regular evaluation of hardware and software suites, investing in flexible, modular solutions that allow for incremental upgrades. Equally important is the continuous development of staff skills through training and professional development, so that teams remain capable of maximizing new tools and technologies as they are introduced.

Finally, neglecting change management can derail even the most technically sound ICT projects. People are at the core of any digital transformation, and staff and stakeholders need to be both prepared for and supportive of new processes or tools. Change resistance can waste resources or even prevent new systems from being adopted at all. Comprehensive change management involves clear communication of project goals, ongoing training, support mechanisms, and active involvement of end-users throughout the project lifecycle. By prioritizing these human factors alongside technical considerations, organizations can facilitate smoother transitions and better overall outcomes.

Pitfall	Proactive Solutions
Underestimating ongoing costs	Incorporate lifecycle budgeting; include recurrent funding lines.
Funding Delays	Develop conservative schedules; engage in interim low-cost initiatives.
Donor concentration risk	Pursue diversified grants and local revenue generation.
Inadequate accountability	Require documentary evidence for all expenditures and approvals.
Technology obsolescence	Plan modular deployments, schedule periodic system reviews.

Cultivating a Culture of Financial Stewardship

Finally, the thesis underscores the importance of organizational culture in embedding strong budget management. Leadership must model prudent financial behaviors, support continual professional development in budget skills, and maintain open communication about financial realities and constraints. By championing transparency, accountability, and collaboration, ICT leaders foster an environment where effective budget practices become an organizational norm rather than a periodic exercise.

Budget management, as explored in the thesis, is not simply an administrative task but a strategic, ongoing process central to the success and sustainability of ICT innovation in resource-constrained environments. With thorough planning, disciplined execution, and a commitment to continuous learning and improvement, ICT leaders can ensure that every dollar invested delivers the greatest possible value and long-term benefit.

Conclusion

Resource and budgetary constraints remain an intrinsic part of the journey toward ICT integration and digital transformation in the Eastern Caribbean and similar settings. These challenges, rather than stopping progress, have acted as a crucible in which effective leadership, strategic innovation, and resilience are forged. The findings and narratives explored throughout this chapter affirm that while the financial and operational hurdles facing ICT project managers are undeniable, they are far from insurmountable. Instead, such challenges prompt a relentless pursuit of new models, adaptable workflows, and a collaborative ethos that ultimately strengthen outcomes for organizations and citizens alike.

As revealed in the thesis, the most impactful ICT leaders in these resource-limited contexts distinguish themselves not only by their technical competencies but also by their vision, flexibility, and commitment to learning. They cultivate a culture that values communication, stakeholder engagement, and proactive problem-solving. Successful leaders prioritize projects by strategic relevance, rigorously monitor and justify expenditures, and understand the importance of phased implementations to manage risk. They are champions of multidisciplinary capacity building, ensuring that teams can respond fluidly to emerging demands and that critical knowledge is both retained and disseminated.

A significant lesson from the research is the critical role of partnerships whether with private sector actors, development agencies, academia, or civil society in expanding both resource availability and organizational know-how. These relationships are most productive when built on mutual trust, clear governance, and the continuous alignment of interests. Long-term donor engagement, synchronized with robust internal revenue-generation strategies, contributes not just to fiscal security, but also to technological relevance and institutional credibility.

The value of creative adaptation permeates every successful case; constraints often catalyze more streamlined, innovative approaches. Embracing open source solutions, restructuring human resource deployment, and maximizing the reuse and life cycle of ICT assets are recurring themes. Equally, the establishment of effective budget management systems and accountability frameworks ensure that limited funds translate to enduring value, rather than transient gains.

The thesis also underscores that sustainable ICT advancement requires ongoing evaluation and willingness to learn from both successes and failures. Effective leaders implement mechanisms for regular financial review, variance analysis, and lessons-learned exercises. They deploy these learnings to continuously strengthen both organizational culture and implementation frameworks.

Ultimately, resource and budget challenges while persistent can serve as drivers of transformation, innovation, and local expertise development. The experiences of the Eastern Caribbean demonstrate that, with the right blend of visionary leadership, adaptive management, and inclusive partnerships, ICT integration can flourish even under the strictest resource limitations. When leaders and project managers embrace these realities with openness and determination, they lay the groundwork for digital ecosystems that yield lasting socioeconomic benefits. The path forward is thus not one of mere survival in adversity, but of thriving through collective intelligence, resilience, and a commitment to seeing challenges as catalysts for sustainable progress.

Chapter 7

Technology Adoption and User Engagement

Engaging End-Users and Building Digital Literacy

Technology adoption within the Caribbean context is a complex and multifaceted process, shaped by social, organizational, and infrastructural challenges. Central to successful ICT integration initiatives is the critical engagement of end-users at every stage of the implementation cycle. Across Grenada and St. Vincent and the Grenadines, IT project managers reported that early participation of end-users — ranging from government employees, business professionals, educators to the general citizenry — fosters a sense of ownership and reduces apprehension toward new digital tools and systems. This engagement is more than a token gesture; it is a foundational strategy that cultivates positive attitudes and long-term buy-in essential for sustainable adoption.

The involvement of end-users begins right at the design and planning phases of technology deployment projects. Several project managers stressed the importance of incorporating insights from users at multiple hierarchical levels, including senior management, middle managers, junior staff, technical specialists, and actual service recipients. For instance, in education, the introduction of electronic testing applications (e-testing) in secondary schools underscored the need for comprehensive digital literacy campaigns. These did not target students alone but extended to supporting teachers and administrative staff, who often serve as gatekeepers and facilitators of technology use in learning environments.

A significant challenge mentioned by participants was the resistance expressed predominantly by older educators, stemming from unfamiliarity with digital tools and inadequate prior training. To tackle this barrier, tailored capacity-building programs became a focal point of the Caribbean Regional Communications Infrastructure Program (CARCIP), an initiative that provided crucial broadband connectivity as well as technological and training resources. These programs emphasized not just the operational use of devices but also pedagogical transformations, guiding teachers to shift their roles from traditional knowledge transmitters toward digital facilitators and coaches. The premise was clear: successful ICT integration depends on educators internalizing that technology use is not about mere device operation but about creatively leveraging these tools to augment instructional methods and enhance student learning outcomes.

Moreover, digital literacy in the Caribbean is not confined to formal education but extends extensively to public services. Citizens must navigate e-government platforms to access vital services such as e-commerce, e-health, and online education. To support this interaction, the establishment of the Government Wide Area Network (GWAN), a fiber-optic backbone developed under

CARCIP, provided high-speed, reliable internet access connecting government offices, educational institutions, and public facilities. This infrastructure serves as a key enabler for end-users across different sectors to confidently engage with digital services, reducing barriers posed by unreliable connectivity and enhancing user experience.

However, fostering digital literacy also requires confronting enduring infrastructural deficiencies. Many schools struggle with inadequate computer lab capacities and insufficient access to computers or mobile devices, limiting the reach and equity of digital education initiatives. For example, despite having classrooms equipped with digital projects, many are unable to accommodate the student population due to space or resource constraints. This gap restricts the practical learning opportunities for students, who may own smartphones but lack proper training in effective device use for educational purposes. The lack of robust infrastructure coupled with limited technology access exacerbates the existing digital divide, particularly affecting rural and under-resourced communities.

To address these challenges, ongoing investments in broadband expansion and targeted digital literacy programs remain essential. Project managers highlighted continuous support and training as pivotal to elevating digital competences across demographic and geographic lines. The strategy includes not only improving physical infrastructure but also designing curricula and community programs aimed at empowering diverse user groups with relevant ICT skills. Public awareness campaigns, workshops, and accessible training modules help to demystify technology and build the confidence of all users, ensuring inclusivity and reducing digital exclusion.

Furthermore, successful engagement approaches often integrate peer learning and community-based training models where knowledgeable early adopters assist others within their networks. This "train-the-trainer" approach has proven effective in disseminating skills widely and creating localized support systems for technology users. It leverages social capital and cultural nuances, making digital literacy efforts contextually relevant and socially accepted.

An important takeaway from the Caribbean experience is that technology adoption thrives when accompanied by holistic efforts spanning infrastructure enhancement, capacity building, cultural change, and continuous user engagement. Digital literacy is not a one-time intervention but a sustained process adapting dynamically to evolving technologies and user needs. Embedding digital skills into educational systems from primary through secondary schools, while also providing adult learning opportunities within communities and workplaces, creates a digitally empowered citizenry capable of harnessing the socio-economic benefits of ICT.

In conclusion, the combination of infrastructural investments like GWAN, inclusive user engagement strategies, and comprehensive digital literacy initiatives forms a cornerstone for the successful adoption of technology across Caribbean societies. Such efforts enable not only individual competence but also catalyze transformative social change, driving economic development, improving public service delivery, and enhancing quality of life for all citizens. The findings underscore that engaging end-user is not solely about technology deployment but about fostering an ecosystem where digital literacy is both a means and an end toward sustainable ICT integration.

Addressing Resistance to Change

Resistance to change is universally recognized as one of the most formidable barriers to the successful adoption of information and communication technology (ICT) within government and business sectors, and this phenomenon is particularly pronounced in the Caribbean context. The doctoral research conducted with IT project managers from Grenada and St. Vincent and the Grenadines revealed a consistent theme: many employees, especially those from older generations, harbor fears related to job security and the complexity of operating new digital technologies. These anxieties contribute to organizational inertia and manifest as either overt opposition or subtle passive pushback against ICT implementations (P7).

The roots of resistance are multifaceted. For many older employees, the prospect of adapting to unfamiliar technologies triggers concerns about being displaced or rendered obsolete. This apprehension results from a combination of factors, including limited prior exposure to digital systems, insufficient training, and the challenge of altering accustomed work routines. Resistance is further compounded by entrenched attitudes and a cultural disposition favoring traditional methods over innovation, which can slow momentum and compromise project timelines (P7; P8).

To effectively mitigate resistance, project managers and organizational leaders must adopt deliberate, strategic communication and engagement approaches. One successful tactic identified in the research involved hands-on demonstrations and word-of-mouth advocacy, wherein staff were afforded opportunities to experience firsthand how ICT solutions could ease their workloads and improve task efficiency, rather than replace their roles (P7). This experiential learning helped dispel fears and gradually cultivated positive perceptions of technology as an enabling tool.

Leadership commitment is paramount in shaping an organizational culture that embraces change. Top management's visible support, through both advocacy and resource allocation, sets a tone that digital transformation is a strategic priority and not merely an operational adjustment. When leaders actively endorse ICT projects and model engagement, they reassure employees that the organization values their roles and is committed to supporting them through transitions (P4). Conversely, a lack of leadership involvement often leaves a vacuum filled by bureaucratic lethargy and resistance grounded in skepticism and fear.

Recognizing the complexity of change dynamics, successful organizations have instituted structured forums and committees to facilitate two-way communication and foster collaboration. The research highlighted the establishment of steering committees and technical working groups, composed of representatives from diverse departments and levels within the organization, as instrumental in reducing resistance (P1; P7). These entities provide platforms for employees to voice concerns, contribute ideas, and receive timely updates, thereby enhancing transparency and ensuring that decision-making processes are inclusive rather than imposed unilaterally.

Such participatory governance mechanisms shift the organization away from siloed operations toward a more integrated culture of cross-functional collaboration. Multiple participants in the study noted that fragmented departmental approaches often led to duplicated efforts, incompatible technologies, and inefficient resource utilization (P3). To counteract this, governments and organizations have employed horizontal integration frameworks, such as the Medium Term Agenda (MTA), to break down silos, foster interdepartmental dialogue, and synchronize ICT initiatives to national development goals (P8; P10).

Cultural transformation is indispensable to overcoming resistance. It involves reorienting organizational norms from risk-aversion toward innovation acceptance, cultivating openness to new ideas, and promoting agility in adapting workflows. Training and capacity-building initiatives support this cultural shift by equipping employees with not only technical skills but also confidence in their ability to navigate change successfully. Participants emphasized that when staff perceive the technology as easy to use and demonstrably beneficial—a key construct of the Technology Acceptance Model (TAM)—their attitudes toward adoption improve significantly (P1; P3).

An essential dimension in addressing resistance is recognizing that change is not a singular event but a process requiring sustained engagement. Implementing ICT solutions often entails evolving organizational roles, developing new competencies, and realigning incentives. Providing ongoing support—through help desks, continuous training, and peer mentoring—helps maintain momentum and alleviates anxiety among users. Furthermore, recognizing and rewarding staff contributions during ICT transformations creates a positive feedback loop, reinforcing willingness and commitment to change (P2; P9).

The research also underscored the importance of proactive change management strategies. These include conducting readiness assessments to gauge employee attitudes prior to deployment, tailoring communication to address specific concerns, and involving users early in pilot phases to gather feedback and foster a sense of ownership. Early and meaningful engagement of end-users demystifies technology, dispels misconceptions, and disenfranchises resistance leaders by integrating their perspectives into solutions (P1; P7).

In conclusion, effectively addressing resistance to change in Caribbean ICT adoption initiatives requires a comprehensive approach that merges strategic leadership with inclusive governance and empathetic communication.

By fostering a culture of collaboration, sustaining capacity-building efforts, and aligning ICT deployment with employee needs and organizational objectives, resistance can be transformed from an impediment into an opportunity for constructive engagement. This holistic approach not only smooths the pathway for technology acceptance but also strengthens organizational resilience, paving the way for sustainable digital transformation aligned with national development priorities.

Training, Support, and Ongoing Capacity Building

Effective adoption of Information and Communication Technologies (ICT) within Caribbean government agencies, educational institutions, and businesses hinges not only on deploying technology but critically on delivering well-structured, continuous training and support that meet the diverse needs of all stakeholders involved. Project managers interviewed in Grenada and St. Vincent and the Grenadines emphasized that training and capacity building are fundamental pillars that sustain ICT implementation success by equipping users and technical staff alike to confidently engage with new systems over the long term.

Despite this clear recognition, multiple constraints impede the smooth provisioning of training services. Chief among these challenges are severely limited training budgets, bureaucratic delays in fund approvals, and the high costs associated with accessing specialized external training. Participant 2 (P2) detailed the procedural obstacle whereby government approval must be sought for any training expenditure exceeding six thousand U.S. dollars—a process that can introduce significant delays, in some cases spanning several months. This sluggish approval mechanism markedly reduces institutional agility in promptly addressing emergent training needs, particularly when multiple employees or entire departments require simultaneous upskilling to support complex ICT projects (P2; P7).

Acknowledging the imperative of developing technical expertise to sustain ICT infrastructures and services, Caribbean governments and partnering agencies have prioritized specialized capacity building for IT personnel. As Participant 10 (P10) described, emphasis has been placed on advanced upskilling in critical domains such as cloud computing, network management, cybersecurity, and interoperability. This technical deepening is vital given the complex nature of modern ICT systems, including Government Wide Area Networks (GWAN), e-government platforms, and integrated public service frameworks. Successful management, maintenance, and evolution of these systems rely heavily on personnel possessing robust competencies in these specialized fields (P10).

Commensurate with focusing on technical staff, considerable attention has been directed toward end-user training tailored to varied skill levels and functional roles. Customized training sessions, often delivered onsite to ensure contextual relevance and accessibility, aim to enhance perceived ease of use (PEOU)—a concept central to the Technology Acceptance Model (TAM). By helping users overcome apprehension and build confidence in operating new technologies, these programs nurture positive attitudes toward ICT adoption and increase overall willingness to engage with digital systems. TAM research consistently demonstrates that heightened PEOU correlates strongly with higher technology acceptance rates, underscoring the strategic importance of investment in user-friendly training initiatives (Davis, 1989; P2; P10).

Capacity building initiatives extend well beyond initial training efforts. Project managers stressed the critical need to institutionalize ongoing support mechanisms, including knowledge-sharing platforms, help desks, and dedicated support teams accessible post-implementation. These resources play a pivotal role in addressing operational issues promptly, reducing user frustration, and mitigating dropout risks—thus fostering continuous use and integration of ICT solutions within daily workflows. Providing such continuous learning ecosystems reflects an understanding that digital literacy is not a one-time achievement but a dynamic, iterative process requiring sustained organizational commitment (P7; P10).

Educational initiatives targeting early schooling stages also serve as foundational steps for building long-term ICT competency. The Caribbean Community's (CARICOM) regional agenda includes guiding frameworks such as the ICT in Education Policy and Acceptable Use Policies for schools, which set standards for safely and effectively integrating technology among students and educators (P3). These policies facilitate the embedding of digital skills development into formal curricula and promote responsible technology use, setting the stage for the cultivation of a digitally literate citizenry ready to thrive in increasingly technology-driven economies.

Nevertheless, infrastructural and resource limitations pose formidable challenges to the full realization of these training and capacity-building goals. Many schools, particularly in rural and underserved communities, suffer from inadequate computer laboratory capacities and insufficient computing devices, restricting hands-on ICT learning experiences. Participant 3 (P3) highlighted that although many students possess personal smartphones, the pedagogical challenge lies in transitioning learners from basic device familiarity toward proficient, purposeful use that includes essential skills such as keyboarding. The existing hardware and spatial constraints in schools undermine efforts to provide equitable digital education, perpetuating the digital divide across demographic and geographic lines (P3).

Responding to these multifaceted challenges necessitates ongoing infrastructure investments aimed at expanding high-speed broadband connectivity and device availability throughout the region. Coupling these infrastructural improvements with targeted, contextually appropriate training programs and public awareness campaigns can help demystify technology, enhance user confidence, and foster inclusivity. Project managers observed that peer learning and community-based "train-the-trainer" models are particularly effective in extending digital literacy in culturally sensitive and socially embedded ways. Empowering early adopters to serve as local champions promotes organic diffusion of skills and knowledge, creating sustainable support networks that cater to diverse community needs (P3).

The Caribbean experience thus illustrates that developing digital literacy is a continuous socio-technical journey involving coordinated investments in infrastructure, policy, education, and skill development. Embedding ICT competence throughout the educational pipeline and extending digital skill development opportunities into workplaces and communities are essential elements of building a resilient, inclusive ICT-enabled society.

In sum, effective ICT adoption in the Caribbean demands a holistic, ongoing commitment to training, capacity building, and user support designed to foster perceived usefulness and ease of use—key drivers of technology acceptance per TAM—and to overcome social and infrastructural barriers. These concerted efforts empower individuals to harness ICT's transformative potential, enabling enhanced public service delivery, economic participation, and educational outcomes, thereby contributing meaningfully to broader regional socio-economic development and digital sovereignty.

Lessons Learned from Implementation Failures and Successes

The doctoral research conducted across Grenada and St. Vincent and the Grenadines revealed several critical lessons emerging from the implementation of ICT projects. These lessons highlight the necessity for structured management, methodological rigor, stakeholder

241

engagement, and infrastructural growth to ensure successful technology adoption and integration in Caribbean contexts.

A primary learning underscores the pivotal role of strategic and structural management. Participants consistently emphasized that the absence of a comprehensive, well-defined, and professionally managed organizational structure hinders ICT project success. Effective implementation depends on governance frameworks aligned with national ICT policies and strategic business objectives. For example, the creation of steering committees and cabinet-level oversight bodies within ministries has been found crucial for enhancing coordination, fostering accountability, and ensuring project coherence. This streamlined management approach prevents fragmented efforts and enables consistent direction during project lifecycles, as repeatedly reported by participants P1 and P11. Without such coordination, projects tend to falter due to conflicting priorities or lack of clear authority.

Closely connected to organizational management is the importance of applying rigorous project management methodologies. Several participants lamented the inconsistent use or complete absence of standardized project management frameworks such as those aligned with PMBOK (Project Management Body of Knowledge). This deficiency often results in erratic project schedules, uncontrolled scope changes, and budget overruns. A recurring recommendation was the adoption of tailored project management frameworks incorporating core elements like risk management, scope control, quality assurance, and clear stakeholder identification. By applying these methodologies, Caribbean ICT initiatives can significantly reduce failure risks and improve delivery consistency. Participant P9 and P11 particularly highlighted how embedding these practices fosters discipline and accountability within ICT projects.

Another crucial lesson centers on ensuring early engagement of end-users and stakeholders to secure buy-in and minimize resistance. The study revealed that projects with proactive inclusion of users in the planning, design, and rollout phases witness greater acceptance and smoother transitions. Engagement strategies involving inclusive consultations, transparent communication, workshops, and feedback mechanisms contribute to cultivating a sense of ownership. Participants P1 and P9 stressed that this early involvement is not simply a courtesy but a strategic necessity to mitigate fears, dispel misconceptions, and align technology functionalities with user needs. This collective ownership aligns well with TAM constructs, as users who perceive systems to be useful and easy to use are more likely to adopt them enthusiastically.

Despite progress, infrastructural gaps remain a considerable barrier limiting the potential benefits of ICT projects. Participants frequently mentioned persistent issues with limited bandwidth, insufficient computing equipment in schools, and inadequate distribution points that undermine service delivery. While projects like the Caribbean Regional Communications Infrastructure Program (CARCIP) began to address these shortcomings by rolling out fiber optic networks and expanding coverage, comprehensive nationwide coverage is still a work in progress. Such infrastructure is foundational for enabling reliable access to e-government, e-learning, and e-commerce platforms. The digital divide, exacerbated by these gaps, disproportionately affects students in rural and marginalized communities, resulting in inequitable service use and slower digital transformation.

Financial challenges introduced another significant lesson. Many ICT projects in the Caribbean rely heavily on donor funding, which often entails lengthy approval procedures and bureaucratic delays. Participants P6 and P7 noted that such delays cause cost escalations and scope creep. For example, a project initially budgeted at three million dollars could increase by almost 60% by the time funds are released. In rapidly changing market conditions, these delays exacerbate risks, undermine momentum, and threaten project viability. The findings suggest that flexible budgeting processes and agile project control mechanisms are needed to adapt financial plans to emerging realities promptly.

Working in organizational silos was cited as a detrimental factor undermining ICT integration efforts. Fragmented operations characterized by departmental or agency-level isolation often lead to duplicated activities, conflicting technical standards, and inefficiencies. Project managers observed that inadequate collaboration and information sharing between ministries and sectors created redundancies and hindered interoperability. To counter this, governments have begun instituting horizontal coordination plans, such as the Medium Term Agenda (MTA), to promote interdepartmental cooperation and joint planning. Such integrative processes enhance resource optimization, reduce fragmentation, and ensure ICT initiatives are aligned and mutually reinforcing.

Legal and policy frameworks were identified as essential enablers for successful ICT adoption. Robust legislation covering acceptable use, data security, e-government transactions, and privacy fosters trust among users and stakeholders. Clear legal guidelines prevent ambiguity in operational responsibilities, secure information, and provide recourse in disputes, thus enhancing system credibility and sustainability. Participants cited policy documents developed at national and regional levels as cornerstones supporting the e-government agenda, providing a foundation for transparent, secure, and accountable ICT deployments.

On the innovation front, the study documented several successful ICT applications that exemplify the tangible benefits of careful planning and strategic implementation. Noteworthy examples include the rollout of electronic document and records management systems (EDRMS), which have streamlined government clerical work, enhanced records security, and reduced processing times. Intelligent transport systems deploying IoT and GPS technologies have improved public safety, passenger convenience, and urban traffic management. The CariSecure law enforcement integration system, connecting fingerprint identification databases across Caribbean jurisdictions, showcases the power of ICT for regional security collaboration. These successes demonstrate the critical role of aligning technology with local needs and capacity while providing sustained user support for adoption.

The research further reinforced the relevance of the Technology Acceptance Model (TAM) in guiding ICT integration in the Caribbean. Core TAM constructs — perceived usefulness (PU), perceived ease of use (PEOU), and user attitude toward use (ATU) — were consistently linked to user acceptance and sustained engagement across projects. When deployed systems are easy to operate and demonstrably enhance job performance or service delivery, public servants, educators, and citizens express positive intentions to use the technology. Conversely, shortcomings in infrastructure, inadequate training, and weak organizational support diminish these perceptions, contributing to resistance or disuse. This theoretical insight accords well with the practical lessons learned, emphasizing the importance of designing user-centric solutions backed by comprehensive capacity building.

In summary, the lessons gleaned from ICT implementations in Grenada and St. Vincent and the Grenadines convey several overarching themes: the indispensable value of structured organizational governance aligned with strategic objectives; the critical need for standardized, localized project management methodologies; the benefits of early and inclusive user engagement to secure buy-in; the imperative to address infrastructural shortfalls; the necessity of flexible financial and project control measures; the importance of overcoming siloed operations through integrated governance; the foundational role of legal and policy frameworks; and the promise inherent in innovative ICT applications that serve public needs. These lessons, grounded in empirical evidence and enriched by theoretical frameworks like TAM, pave the way for enhancing ICT project success rates and scaling positive social and economic impacts across the Caribbean.

Conclusion

The adoption of technology and successful user engagement in information and communication technology (ICT) projects within Caribbean contexts depend on a multifaceted and strategic approach. Central to this is the active engagement and empowerment of end-users through well-designed training programs and sustained digital literacy initiatives. This approach ensures that users—from government officials and business professionals to educators and citizens—gain the knowledge, skills, and confidence necessary to interact effectively with new digital systems. By fostering digital literacy at various levels, projects improve the likelihood that end-users will embrace and utilize technologies to their full potential, which is vital for sustaining positive outcomes.

Another critical dimension involves addressing resistance to change, a frequent barrier in ICT adoption within government and business sectors. Strategies that emphasize inclusiveness, promote transparent and ongoing communication, and secure strong leadership support emerge as effective mechanisms to overcome apprehension and inertia often experienced by users. Leadership's visible commitment to digital transformation creates an environment that reassures employees, reduces fears related to job security, and fosters motivation to adapt to new systems. Carefully constructed forums and collaborative committees ensure stakeholders at all levels can voice concerns, contribute ideas, and stay informed, thereby reducing resistance through participation and shared ownership.

Ongoing capacity building is essential to adapt to the rapidly evolving technological landscape. Effective ICT adoption demands not only initial technical training but continuous development that extends across the lifecycle of technology deployment. This includes institutionalizing support mechanisms such as knowledge-sharing platforms, help desks, and expert support teams. These components facilitate prompt resolution of operational issues, reduce user frustration, and prevent dropout, thus sustaining system use and maximizing benefits over time. Moreover, embedding ICT competencies early in educational curricula—supported by coherent policy frameworks and guidelines—is fundamental to cultivating a digitally fluent populace prepared for future socio-economic demands.

Learning from past experiences in implementation yields valuable insights critical for enhancing project success rates. Establishing structured and professionally managed organizational frameworks aligned with national ICT strategies acts as a foundation for effective governance and coordination. The consistent application of project management methodologies tailored to local contexts, incorporating best practices in risk management, scope control, and quality assurance, directly impacts project delivery and outcomes. Early and active engagement of users throughout the development lifecycle fosters ownership and reduces resistance, aligning technology solutions more closely to end-user needs.

Yet, infrastructure gaps — including limitations in bandwidth, device availability, and equitable distribution of network access — persistently restrict the reach and effectiveness of ICT initiatives. Projects like the Caribbean Regional Communications Infrastructure Program (CARCIP) aim to bridge these divides, but comprehensive, widespread infrastructure remains a work in progress. Financial complexities, particularly in donor-funded projects subject to approval delays and dynamic market conditions, underscore the necessity for flexible budgetary mechanisms and agile project management practices to mitigate risks and cost overruns.

Equally important is overcoming organizational silos that impede coordination and collaboration. Fragmented operations often result in duplicated efforts, inconsistent technical standards, and waste of resources. Integrated governance approaches promote horizontal cooperation across ministries, agencies, and sectors, fostering the efficient use of ICT assets and holistic progress. Complementing these operational aspects are robust legal and policy frameworks that provide the necessary regulatory environment to secure data integrity, guide e-government practices, and build user trust.

Innovative ICT applications have demonstrated tangible social and administrative benefits. Systems such as electronic document and records management, intelligent transportation networks, and regional law enforcement platforms exemplify how technology can improve efficiency, safety, and service delivery. These successes affirm the value of aligning technological advancements with practical local needs and securing user support.

Throughout these multifaceted processes, the Technology Acceptance Model (TAM) provides a valuable theoretical lens, emphasizing that the perceived usefulness and ease of use of technology, along with positive user attitudes, strongly influence adoption rates and sustained engagement. Investments in training and supportive infrastructure enhance these perceptions, enabling users to recognize the practical benefits of ICT in improving job performance and daily activities.

By integrating these insights—engagement, capacity building, resistance management, governance, infrastructure, and theory-informed design—Caribbean ICT projects can substantially improve their effectiveness, social impact, and sustainability. These lessons are essential not only for the Caribbean region but also offer guidance for other developing contexts striving to harness technology's transformative potential for socio-economic advancement.

Chapter 8

Measuring Impact and Ensuring Sustainability

Introduction

The successful implementation of information and communication technology (ICT) projects in the Caribbean marks a crucial milestone in harnessing the transformative potential of digital innovation for socio-economic progress. However, reaching this milestone is merely the beginning of a much broader journey. To ensure that ICT initiatives deliver lasting benefits, it is essential not only to implement projects effectively but also to rigorously measure their performance, assess their impact, and develop strategies that guarantee their sustainability over time. Without these critical steps, the envisioned improvements in governance, economic participation, education, and social inclusion risk falling short of their full potential.

This chapter seeks to deepen the understanding of how ICT projects can be optimally managed beyond deployment by exploring effective practices and frameworks for ongoing monitoring, evaluation, and sustainability. In particular, it focuses on the Eastern Caribbean context, where unique geographic, economic, and institutional realities shape the digital transformation landscape. Drawing from insights gained in preceding chapters, lessons from practitioner experiences, scholarly research, and international best practices, this chapter advocates for a life cycle

251

management approach to ICT integration projects. Such an approach emphasizes continuous learning, adaptive management, and strategic alignment with broader regional development goals.

The content is organized around three core thematic pillars essential to achieving enduring success in ICT initiatives. The first theme examines the setting and tracking of key performance indicators (KPIs) as vital tools for gauging project effectiveness, identifying bottlenecks, and enabling evidence-based decision-making. Establishing clear metrics aligned with stakeholder expectations permits organizations to measure progress and outcomes in a transparent and accountable manner. The second theme addresses the critical need to embed sustainability into ICT efforts. This includes organizational capacity building, financial planning, infrastructure maintenance, and the adoption of technologies that allow for scalability and adaptability amid rapidly evolving digital environments. Emphasizing sustainability ensures that projects do not become one-off investments but instead evolve as integral components of institutional and societal frameworks. The third theme explores strategies for scaling successful ICT initiatives beyond initial pilot phases to achieve broader impact. This entails fostering collaboration across Caribbean islands, knowledge sharing among practitioners, policy coherence, and leveraging regional integration mechanisms that pool resources and expertise. Scaling enables the diffusion of innovation to underserved areas and populations, thereby widening digital access and inclusivity.

Each section illuminates the challenges inherent in the Caribbean ICT project environment, including infrastructural disparities, resource constraints, governance complexities, and cultural factors influencing technology adoption. Importantly, practical strategies and lessons learned are drawn from the Caribbean experience, supported by illustrative examples that showcase both successes and areas for improvement. These insights aim to equip ICT managers, policymakers, and stakeholders with actionable guidance to enhance project performance, reinforce sustainability, and amplify positive socio-economic outcomes across the region.

In summary, this chapter contributes to advancing the discourse on ICT project life cycle management by articulating a comprehensive framework for monitoring, sustainability, and scaling. By doing so, it underscores the imperative to move beyond simply delivering technology solutions to cultivating resilient, inclusive digital ecosystems that drive long-term development in the Eastern Caribbean and beyond.

Setting and Tracking Key Performance Indicators (KPIs)

The Role of KPIs in ICT Project Success

Setting and tracking key performance indicators (KPIs) is a fundamental practice in the governance and management of ICT projects, especially within the Caribbean context where resource constraints, institutional variability, and socio-technical complexities abound. KPIs serve as vital tools that translate abstract project goals into quantifiable, actionable metrics, thereby enabling a clear evaluation of how well an ICT project is fulfilling its intended outcomes. For ICT projects in developing regions like the Caribbean, effective KPIs are not merely administrative instruments but critical drivers of project transparency, stakeholder engagement, and impact realization.

Within Caribbean ICT initiatives, KPIs assume multiple important roles that collectively contribute to project success. First, KPIs provide project managers and involved stakeholders with a dynamic, real-time lens through which to monitor progress toward established goals. This ongoing visibility facilitates early detection of challenges or deviations from plans, allowing timely corrective actions and minimizing risks of failure or cost overruns. Second, KPIs enable and promote data-driven decision-making processes whereby empirical evidence guides strategic adjustments and operational improvements throughout the life cycle of the project. Third, a well-articulated KPI framework supports the justification of investments in ICT by quantifying the social, economic, and operational benefits attained. By clearly demonstrating value-added outcomes, such as enhanced public service delivery, economic empowerment through e-commerce, or improved educational engagement via e-learning platforms, KPIs contribute to securing and sustaining financial, political, and community support. Lastly, KPIs establish foundational mechanisms for accountability and transparency, ensuring that project implementers are answerable to government bodies, funding agencies, and the wider public throughout the implementation phase and beyond.

Despite their vital importance, defining effective KPIs for ICT projects in the Caribbean is a complex and nuanced endeavor. The region exhibits diverse institutional arrangements, fragmented governance structures, and a broad range of ICT adoption maturity levels across countries and sectors. These factors compound the challenge of designing KPIs that are simultaneously measurable, relevant, and sensitive to local socio-economic realities. Practical difficulties such as inconsistent data availability, limited capacity for systematic data collection and analysis, and the positioning of ICT projects within broader political and cultural contexts complicate indicator design further. Consequently, a balanced KPI framework is necessary—one that encompasses a spectrum of quantitative and qualitative metrics capturing inputs (e.g., budget allocation, training hours), process efficiency (e.g., adherence to project timelines, user engagement levels), outputs (e.g., deployment completion, service accessibility), outcomes (e.g., user satisfaction, adoption rates), and longer-term impacts on socio-economic development and institutional capacity. By embedding a holistic evaluation schema reflective of multidimensional project goals, stakeholders can derive a comprehensive understanding that transcends mere activity monitoring to encompass transformative benefits.

Operationalizing KPIs within Caribbean ICT projects mandates the purposeful involvement of all key stakeholders, including policymakers, project managers, technical teams, users, and beneficiaries. Stakeholder engagement in KPI selection is critical to aligning performance metrics with national development agendas and regional integration efforts, fostering a shared vision and ownership of success criteria. A combination of quantitative KPIs with qualitative feedback mechanisms enriches performance appraisal by incorporating user attitudes, behavioral intentions, cultural acceptance factors, and contextual challenges, which are highly relevant in technology acceptance models underlying ICT adoption. Moreover, leveraging ICT solutions themselves to automate data collection, facilitate real-time reporting, and enable interactive dashboards enhances monitoring efficacy but demands concurrent attention to capacity building and infrastructure readiness. Embedding KPI assessment into regular project review cycles supports adaptive management by allowing continuous recalibration of strategies, reprioritization of resources, and scaling-up of effective interventions. Ultimately, establishing credible, context-sensitive, and actionable KPIs fosters a culture of accountability and continuous learning in ICT project management.

Through deliberate and sustained focus on KPIs, Caribbean ICT projects can move beyond episodic successes toward sustained digital transformation capable of widening digital inclusion, enhancing public administration effectiveness, and generating broad-based socio-economic development. KPIs not only measure achievements; they shape processes, inform policies, and guide investments that collectively contribute to resilient, adaptable, and impactful ICT ecosystems across the Eastern Caribbean.

Designing Relevant KPIs

At the core of developing effective key performance indicators (KPIs) lies the fundamental principle of alignment. KPIs must be intrinsically linked to the specific goals of the ICT project and the actual needs of users and stakeholders. This alignment ensures that the indicators serve not merely as abstract numerical targets but as meaningful measures that accurately reflect progress and outcomes relevant to all project participants. In Caribbean ICT initiatives, this alignment is especially crucial due to the region's distinctive socio-economic and infrastructural realities, which demand that KPIs balance technical achievement, user engagement, and broader societal impact.

Given the multifaceted nature of ICT projects in the Caribbean, an effective KPI framework incorporates a diverse yet coherent set of quantitative and qualitative indicators. These indicators collectively capture the technical performance of systems, levels of user adoption and engagement, the development of organizational and individual capacity, as well as economic and social benefits arising from ICT deployment. This balanced approach allows for a comprehensive evaluation, ensuring that projects are not judged solely on technical delivery but on their integration into social contexts, acceptance by end-users, and contribution to economic growth and public welfare.

Technical performance KPIs form the foundation of any ICT project's metrics and assess system reliability, efficiency, and availability. Commonly measured parameters include system uptime, which reflects the accessibility and stability of the infrastructure; data throughput and network latency, indicating the quality and speed of data transmission; the number of users served, showing system reach; and overall service availability. These metrics provide tangible evidence about whether the ICT infrastructure meets design specifications and fulfills its operational role, which is critical in Caribbean settings where infrastructure resilience often confronts natural disaster risks and uneven development challenges.

While technical success is foundational, adoption and usage KPIs reveal the extent to which technology solutions resonate with and are actively used by intended recipients. These include the percentage of target users adopting the technology, the frequency with which users engage with systems, user satisfaction scores gathered through surveys or interviews, and transactional volumes processed via digital platforms. For Caribbean ICT projects, such as e-government services or educational platforms, these KPIs highlight issues of accessibility, usability, and cultural acceptance, which can vary widely across islands and social groups. Monitoring user engagement informs managers about the real-world effectiveness of a solution and guides adjustments to improve experience and uptake.

Capacity building remains a cornerstone in ensuring the sustainability of ICT initiatives, captured through KPIs such as the number of personnel trained, demonstrable improvements in digital literacy, and documented enhancements in organizational ICT competencies. In many Caribbean countries, where tight budgets and limited skilled labor pose impediments to digital transformation, these indicators serve to mark progress in empowering individuals and institutions. For example, tracking the skills development of government staff or educators implementing e-learning technologies provides critical insight into the human capital dimension necessary to maintain and evolve ICT investments.

Economic impact KPIs strengthen the justification for ICT projects by quantifying improvements in efficiency and economic opportunity. Cost savings realized through automated processes, revenue generation enabled by new ICT-enabled services, and the creation of jobs in ICT sectors are tangible outcomes that resonate deeply with policy makers and funders. In the Caribbean context, where economic diversification is a strategic imperative, such KPIs demonstrate how ICT can serve as a catalyst for entrepreneurship, market expansion, and integration into global value chains.

Finally, social impact KPIs examine the broader, often intangible, benefits of ICT initiatives. These include improved access to education and health services facilitated by ICT, heightened citizen engagement with government, and enhanced perceptions of government transparency and accountability. Projects targeting digital inclusion among marginalized groups, rural communities, or schools often rely on social impact indicators to measure success beyond mere technical delivery. For instance, increasing the proportion of students accessing e-learning platforms or tracking the usage of digital health resources in rural areas exemplify how social impact KPIs connect technology deployment to real improvements in quality of life.

In practice, Caribbean IT project managers have stressed the necessity of tailoring KPI sets to reflect local priorities and specific project aims. For example, in government-focused projects, KPIs might emphasize improvements in service delivery speed, expansion of broadband access to underserved rural populations, or the integration of ICT in educational curricula. In contrast, projects aimed at business development might focus more heavily on economic metrics such as job creation or e-commerce transaction volumes. Such contextual customization of KPIs ensures meaningful measurement that drives relevant management action and policy formulation.

Designing relevant KPIs also requires addressing region-specific challenges such as data availability and quality, varying levels of ICT literacy, and infrastructural limitations. Collaborative engagement with stakeholders—including government officials, technical specialists, end users, and community representatives—facilitates the development of KPIs that are practical, culturally sensitive, and feasible to monitor. Incorporating qualitative measures such as user experience feedback and satisfaction surveys alongside quantitative data creates a richer evaluative environment that captures the nuances of technology adoption and impact in Caribbean societies.

Moreover, the iterative review and refinement of KPIs throughout the project life cycle are essential components of adaptive management. Emerging issues, shifting priorities, and lessons learned should be reflected in KPI updates, ensuring continuous alignment with strategic objectives and responsiveness to user needs. Utilizing ICT-enabled data collection and reporting tools can enhance the timeliness and accuracy of KPI monitoring, although advancing digital infrastructure and capacity remain prerequisites.

Ultimately, well-designed and contextually relevant KPIs are more than measurement tools—they are enablers of accountability, learning, and strategic management. They empower Caribbean ICT projects to demonstrate clear value, foster stakeholder trust, and sustain momentum toward inclusive digital development. By embedding these practices, Caribbean nations can better capture the full promise of ICT to transform societies, drive economic progress, and improve governance and public service delivery.

Tools and Methods for Tracking KPIs

Tracking key performance indicators (KPIs) effectively is integral to the sound management and evaluation of ICT projects, forming the backbone of monitoring and evaluation (M&E) activities that ensure projects meet goals and produce intended benefits. Establishing robust M&E systems that are seamlessly integrated within the governance structures of ICT initiatives is essential for providing continuous visibility into project progress, outcomes, and impact. Such systems help capture a comprehensive and timely picture of technical performance, user engagement, capacity development, financial management, and socio-economic effects, which collectively inform decision-making, risk mitigation, and adaptive strategies.

In the Caribbean, specifically within the Eastern Caribbean nations such as Grenada and St. Vincent and the Grenadines, practitioners reflected on their experiences utilizing a multi-faceted array of tools and methods tailored to their particular context's infrastructural, institutional, and geographic realities. A key component has been the deployment of automated digital dashboards directly interfaced with network management and operational systems. These dashboards provide near real-time data relating to technical KPIs, including system uptime, network latency, bandwidth utilization, error rates, and traffic statistics. Such automation enables ICT managers to rapidly detect service interruptions or performance anomalies, facilitating immediate troubleshooting and preventative maintenance essential for sustaining critical infrastructure in often resource-limited Caribbean environments.

Alongside automated metrics, qualitative data collection tools such as structured surveys, semi-structured interviews, and focus group discussions have been employed extensively. These methods gather in-depth feedback from end users about system usability, satisfaction, perceived usefulness, and barriers to adoption. By capturing user perspectives, project teams can identify nuanced socio-cultural and operational issues that may not be evident through quantitative technical data alone. For instance, community-based focus groups in rural or dispersed island settings have surfaced challenges related to digital literacy, infrastructure accessibility, and cultural acceptance—factors crucial to shaping effective user-centric improvements and capacity-building interventions.

Institutional reporting mechanisms form another vital pillar in KPI tracking. Formal procedures embedded within organizational workflows document progress on non-technical metrics, such as training completions, budget execution, procurement milestones, compliance with data governance policies, and achievement of milestones aligned with strategic plans. Regular submission and review of these reports provide governmental oversight bodies and project sponsors with essential accountability and transparency, enabling timely escalation and resolution of issues involving human resources, project finance, or operational bottlenecks.

To assess outcomes beyond operational indicators, periodic impact evaluations are conducted typically at mid-term and project completion stages. These assessments utilize mixed-methods approaches combining quantitative data analysis with case studies and community consultations to evaluate the broader social, economic, and institutional impacts of ICT initiatives. Such evaluations explore how projects have contributed to enhanced access to services, economic empowerment, governance improvements, and digital inclusion across varied Caribbean demographic and geographic segments.

A persistent challenge encountered in the Caribbean origin point revolves around reliable data collection across geographically scattered and often rural user populations. Limited internet connectivity, infrastructural fragility, and variable ICT literacy impede purely digital data acquisition efforts and threaten data completeness and accuracy. To surmount these challenges, hybrid data collection strategies have proven effective. These approaches blend automated digital analytics with manual data gathering techniques, including paper-based surveys, telephone interviews, and community-led monitoring by trained local representatives. This hybrid modality not only augments data quality and coverage but also fosters community engagement and trust, which are crucial for sustainable monitoring regimes in island contexts.

Finally, the implementation of advanced ICT tools to facilitate KPI tracking must be accompanied by capacity-building initiatives targeting data management skills, analytical competencies, and reporting capabilities of project teams and institutional stakeholders. Investment in training on using mobile data collection apps, cloud-based data aggregation platforms, and real-time visualization interfaces maximizes the utility of monitoring systems. However, such technological sophistication needs to be introduced incrementally and aligned with the existing infrastructure and human resource realities of Caribbean ICT environments.

In sum, the suite of tools and methods for tracking KPIs in Caribbean ICT projects reflects a pragmatic but evolving balance of automated digital monitoring, participatory qualitative data collection, institutional process reporting, and adaptive mixed-methods evaluation. When embedded within structured governance frameworks that prioritize transparency, accountability, and continuous learning, these systems equip ICT projects to realize improved performance, sustainability, and scalability—delivering tangible socio-economic benefits to Caribbean societies.

Examples of KPIs in Caribbean ICT Projects

In the pursuit of effective monitoring and evaluation of ICT projects within the Caribbean, policymakers and project managers have prioritized the development of tailored KPIs that embrace both operational outputs and broader social and economic impacts. By doing so, they seek to quantify progress and communicate tangible value to funders, stakeholders, and communities, thereby strengthening ongoing support and ensuring sustainability of digital initiatives.

A prominent example lies in broadband expansion efforts, wherein one widely used KPI is the percentage increase in household coverage of high-speed internet relative to baseline levels prior to project launch. This metric captures not only the physical reach of infrastructure investments but also serves as an indicator of improved digital access for citizens, especially in underserved rural and remote areas. Tracking coverage expansion provides clear evidence of infrastructural enhancement efforts, directly associated with greater connectivity and potential for socio-economic uplift through access to e-services and digital platforms.

In the arena of e-government services, KPIs focus on measurable improvements in service delivery that directly influence citizen engagement and government efficiency. Common indicators include the number of online transactions completed successfully on a monthly basis, reflecting both system usage and functionality, and the reduction in turnaround time for processing government services, which demonstrates enhanced responsiveness and streamlining of administrative procedures. Such KPIs offer quantitative benchmarks to assess whether e-government platforms are effectively reducing bureaucratic bottlenecks and improving user experience, thereby fostering greater trust and adoption.

E-learning platforms also feature prominently in ICT integration projects within the region, given education's critical role in socio-economic development. KPIs in this domain might include student login frequency, which gauges user engagement and system penetration, alongside improvements in digital test scores, providing evidence of learning outcomes facilitated by technology. Furthermore, the completion rates of teacher certification programs related to digital pedagogy serve as key indicators of capacity building, highlighting the preparedness of educators to effectively integrate ICT tools into teaching and learning processes.

The digitalization of business operations represents another critical focus area. Here, pertinent KPIs encompass the number of micro, small, and medium enterprises (MSMEs) adopting digital payment solutions, reflecting progress in modernizing transactional processes and financial inclusion. Additionally, the percentage increase in e-commerce sales within target sectors captures the economic benefits of ICT adoption and the growth of digital marketplaces. These measures underscore the direct link between technology deployments and enhanced business performance, competitiveness, and market reach.

By carefully selecting KPIs that resonate with both operational dimensions — such as system uptime, user adoption, and training completions — and impact-related dimensions encompassing economic and social transformation, project managers are better positioned to articulate the value generated by ICT investments. This comprehensive approach to performance measurement enhances transparency and accountability, informs adaptive management throughout the project life cycle, and importantly, supports the case for sustained funding and policy backing.

Moreover, these KPIs align with the core constructs of the Technology Acceptance Model (TAM), reflecting perceived usefulness and ease of use, as user engagement and satisfaction serve as proxies for technology acceptance in real-world deployment. Successful application of TAM in designing and evaluating these metrics affirms their relevance in capturing critical influencers of adoption and sustained ICT integration.

In summary, the strategic use of these examples of KPIs across broadband, e-government, education, and business digitalization efforts exemplify a methodical commitment to embedding evaluative rigor within Caribbean ICT projects. Such practices empower project teams and regional policymakers to measure progress meaningfully, enhance learning and improvement, and extend the transformative impact of ICT toward inclusive digital economies and improved citizen livelihoods throughout the Caribbean.

Ensuring Long-Term Sustainability of ICT Projects

Understanding Sustainability Dimensions

Sustainability in ICT projects transcends the mere technical longevity or operational maintenance of deployed systems; it embodies a multifaceted concept that includes financial, institutional, social, and environmental dimensions. For ICT initiatives in the Caribbean to succeed beyond their initial implementation phase, it is imperative to address each of these dimensions holistically. Failure to do so risks premature project obsolescence, underutilization, or collapse, thereby negating the substantial investments made and the potential socio-economic benefits these projects aim to deliver.

Technical Sustainability forms the foundational pillar of ICT longevity and involves designing system architectures and infrastructures that are robust yet adaptable. These systems must be scalable to accommodate growing user bases and evolving service demands, interoperable with existing and future technologies to avoid vendor lock-in and fragmentation, maintainable with clear guidelines and resources for updates and troubleshooting, and resilient to the fast-paced changes characteristic of the ICT landscape. In the Caribbean context, where natural disasters such as hurricanes pose recurrent risks, technical designs must incorporate disaster resilience features, including redundant connectivity, backup power solutions, and rapid recovery mechanisms. The adoption of open standards and modular frameworks further enhances long-term usability and eases integration with emerging technologies, critical for sustaining digital transformation in a resource-constrained region.

Financial Sustainability addresses the critical necessity for securing ongoing funding and managing costs beyond the initial donor grants, capital investments, or government budget allocations that typically finance ICT project rollouts. Caribbean ICT projects often begin with externally funded infrastructure or pilot initiatives but falter without clear financial models for operational continuity. Sustainable projects explore diverse revenue streams such as cost recovery through user fees or service tariffs, subscription models, and partnerships with the private sector through public-private partnerships (PPP). Financial planning must also consider recurrent expenses, including system maintenance, software licensing, user support, and training programs. Establishing transparent budgeting processes and financial oversight enables stakeholders to anticipate funding needs and mobilize resources efficiently, thereby preventing service interruptions and degradation.

Organizational Sustainability pertains to the internal capacities, structures, and governance mechanisms crucial for embedding ICT projects into existing institutions. This dimension emphasizes building local expertise through continuous capacity development, fostering institutional ownership where stakeholders perceive ICT as integral to their operations, and developing effective leadership committed to digital transformation. For Caribbean governments and organizations, cultivating a culture that values innovation, embraces change, and incorporates ICT governance into strategic planning is essential for longevity. Enhancing institutional frameworks may involve formalizing ICT units within ministries, establishing multi-stakeholder steering committees, defining clear roles and responsibilities, and adopting project management methodologies aligned with regional needs. Without such organizational embedding, ICT projects risk being viewed as isolated technical endeavors rather than drivers of systemic change.

Social Sustainability captures the human and community factors ensuring that ICT solutions remain relevant, accepted, and actively used over time. This dimension recognizes that technology adoption hinges on meaningful engagement with end users, including extensive training, awareness campaigns, and culturally sensitive implementation strategies. In the Caribbean, social diversity, varying digital literacy levels, and resistance to change present notable challenges. Continuous community involvement from project inception through post-deployment phases ensures that ICT services reflect users' preferences and needs. Providing ongoing training and support empowers users, fostering confidence and reducing barriers to adoption. Moreover, addressing social equity considerations helps bridge digital divides, ensuring marginalized or rural populations benefit equally. Projects that embed feedback loops and adapt to evolving social contexts are more likely to maintain sustained user engagement and generate lasting socio-economic impact.

In sum, the sustainability of ICT projects in the Caribbean requires a comprehensive approach that integrates technical robustness, financial viability, organizational capacity, and social acceptance. By prioritizing these interconnected dimensions, project managers and policymakers can enhance the likelihood that ICT initiatives not only survive but thrive, delivering inclusive digital services that underpin economic growth, improved governance, education, health, and social development across the region.

Challenges to Sustainability in the Caribbean

The sustainability of ICT projects in the Caribbean is frequently compromised by a multifaceted set of interrelated barriers that extend beyond technical concerns to include financial, institutional, cultural, and governance challenges. Participants in this study, drawn from practitioners and stakeholders deeply acquainted with the region's ICT landscape, highlighted several critical obstacles that impede long-term sustainability and threaten the continuity and success of ICT initiatives.

Funding Gaps emerged as the most prominent concern. While initial project launches often benefit from donor support, government allocations, or international funding mechanisms, many Caribbean ICT projects face significant shortfalls in securing ongoing financial resources necessary for maintenance, upgrades, system enhancements, and capacity-building activities. This scarcity of sustainable funding translates into interruptions in service delivery, delayed technology refresh cycles, and inadequate user training programs—all of which undermine the progress achieved during project implementation. The challenge is compounded by fluctuating economic conditions, budgetary constraints typical of small island economies, and competing government priorities, which can deprioritize ICT projects post-launch despite their potential societal benefits.

Capacity Constraints constitute another pervasive impediment, specifically the shortage of skilled personnel endowed with the expertise required for the operation, troubleshooting, and progression of complex ICT systems. Within the Caribbean public sector and private enterprise alike, the limited pool of ICT professionals, coupled with frequent brain drain to larger economies, constrains the ability to sustain institutional knowledge and deliver responsive support. Many government units struggle to offer continual training programs or retain talent able to adapt to evolving technology environments. This capacity deficit impairs critical functions such as system maintenance, user support, and security management, ultimately increasing vulnerability to failures and decreasing user confidence and adoption.

The rapid pace of Technological Change further complicates sustainability. ICT systems implemented today risk early obsolescence amid the accelerating development of new platforms, standards, and innovations such as cloud computing, artificial intelligence, blockchain, and the Internet of Things (IoT). Without adaptive governance frameworks, flexible infrastructure architectures, and proactive upgrade pathways, Caribbean ICT initiatives may become outdated quickly, diminishing investment returns and discouraging continual use. The necessity of balancing innovation adoption with stability remains a delicate act, especially in environments constrained by limited resources and infrastructural rigidity.

The Caribbean also faces the challenge of Fragmented Policy Environments. The lack of cohesive, harmonized regional ICT policies and regulatory frameworks leads to duplication of efforts, inconsistent standards, and inefficiencies in resource utilization. Varied policy approaches among islands within organizations such as CARICOM and the OECS limit the potential for economies of scale and shared learning. Some countries have advanced more rapidly in ICT governance than others, leading to uneven implementation landscapes. Coordination difficulties between ministries, agencies, and international development partners generate gaps in strategic alignment, funding prioritization, and accountability mechanisms, thereby impairing the systemic sustainability of ICT projects.

Moreover, Cultural Resistance remains a subtle yet formidable barrier. Ingrained skepticism or inertia toward the adoption of new technologies endures among certain stakeholder segments, particularly among older workers and traditionalists within public administration and educational institutions. Concerns range from fear of job loss due to automation, lack of familiarity or trust in digital systems, to perceptions of increased complexity and workload. This resistance often manifests as passive disengagement or active opposition, slowing the diffusion of technology and complicating capacity-building efforts. Overcoming cultural resistance requires sustained user training, transparent communication strategies, and participatory approaches that promote ownership and trust.

Taken together, these challenges require comprehensive, coordinated responses that address not only technical factors but also the broader socio-economic, institutional, and policy environments. Successful sustainability frameworks in the Caribbean need to incorporate mechanisms for reliable financial resourcing, continuous professional development, dynamic technology governance, integrated regional policy harmonization, and culturally informed stakeholder engagement. Addressing these barriers holistically can unlock the full potential of ICT projects to foster inclusive digital economies, resilient public services, and sustainable regional development.

Strategies to Enhance Sustainability

Ensuring the long-term sustainability of ICT projects in the Caribbean requires a deliberate and multifaceted strategy that goes beyond the initial design and deployment phases. One of the foundational strategies involves developing comprehensive sustainability plans that articulate clear pathways for financial viability, capacity building, risk mitigation, and technology upgrades. Such plans must detail not only the sources of ongoing funding—including public budget commitments, donor support, and innovative financing mechanisms—but also address the human resource development necessary for maintaining and evolving ICT infrastructure. Importantly, sustainability plans need to incorporate scheduled technology refresh cycles to prevent obsolescence and ensure adaptability to the rapidly changing digital landscape. Effective risk management within these plans anticipates potential operational, financial, and technological challenges, enabling proactive responses that safeguard project outcomes and reinforce stakeholder confidence.

Capacity building and knowledge transfer constitute critical pillars supporting sustainability, particularly in Caribbean countries facing talent shortages and brain drain. Intensive and continuous training programs are vital to cultivate and retain skilled ICT personnel who can support operations, troubleshoot issues, and drive innovation. The 'train-the-trainer' model has proven effective in this regional context by empowering local experts to disseminate skills across organizations, thereby institutionalizing knowledge and reducing dependency on external consultants. Beyond technical proficiency, capacity-building initiatives also need to focus on managerial and governance competencies essential for overseeing ICT projects within complex institutional environments. Embedding knowledge transfer mechanisms ensures resilience and continuity, even amid staff turnover or organizational changes.

Engaging communities and stakeholders early and consistently throughout the project lifecycle is another strategy key to sustainability. Active stakeholder involvement fosters a sense of ownership, which is critical for ICT solutions to remain relevant, supported, and utilized over time. In the Caribbean, where diverse cultural and socio-economic contexts influence technology adoption, participatory approaches help tailor solutions to local needs and conditions, reducing resistance and building trust. Transparent communication, inclusive feedback mechanisms, and stakeholder collaboration not only improve project design and implementation but also empower users as partners in sustaining ICT initiatives. This engagement promotes social sustainability by bridging digital divides and fostering equitable access.

Leveraging public-private partnerships (PPPs) provides a valuable strategy to pool resources, expertise, and funding for delivering scalable and high-quality ICT infrastructure and services. Given the financial constraints many Caribbean governments face, PPPs offer pragmatic avenues to share costs and risks while benefiting from private sector efficiencies and innovation. Strategic PPPs can accelerate infrastructure deployment, enhance service delivery, and create mutually beneficial value propositions. For example, partnerships involving telecommunications providers and government agencies have been instrumental in expanding broadband access and enabling e-government services in the region. A well-structured PPP framework ensures alignment of objectives, clear governance, and equitable sharing of benefits, all of which underpin project sustainability.

Promoting regional cooperation and standardization is a further crucial strategy for overcoming fragmentation and achieving economies of scale across Caribbean island states. Harmonizing standards, regulatory policies, and operational procedures across countries reduces duplication, facilitates interoperability, and strengthens collective bargaining power. Regional integration bodies such as CARICOM and the Organization of Eastern Caribbean States (OECS) play pivotal roles in fostering collaboration by coordinating ICT policy harmonization, shared infrastructure development, and cross-border knowledge exchange. Such cooperation enhances the sustainability of ICT projects by enabling resource optimization, consistent quality standards, and coordinated responses to common challenges, ultimately accelerating the digital transformation agenda at a regional scale.

Finally, embedding ICT governance within organizational and institutional frameworks ensures that responsibility, accountability, and authority for ICT initiatives are clearly defined and supported. Establishing dedicated ICT units or divisions within government ministries or large organizations provides the institutional home for overseeing the lifecycle of ICT projects, from planning and implementation to maintenance and evaluation. Effective governance encompasses policy development, performance monitoring, and alignment with national and regional digital strategies. Leadership commitment, both political and managerial, is essential to sustain momentum, navigate challenges, and institutionalize digital practices. Embedding ICT governance helps overcome the risks of siloed efforts, resource misallocation, and shifting priorities, thereby enhancing the durability and impact of ICT investments.

Together, these strategies constitute an integrated approach that addresses the technical, financial, organizational, and social complexities inherent in sustaining ICT projects in the Caribbean. When thoughtfully applied, they empower project managers, policymakers, and stakeholders to build resilient, adaptable, and inclusive digital ecosystems that drive long-term socio-economic development and regional integration.

Case Example: Sustainability Measures in Caribbean ICT Initiatives

The Caribbean Regional Communications Infrastructure Program (CARCIP) stands as a flagship regional initiative exemplifying robust sustainability strategies explicitly embedded across its project phases. CARCIP's approach integrated comprehensive capacity building, recognizing that technical infrastructure alone is inadequate without the concurrent development of human capital and institutional expertise. Trainings, knowledge-sharing workshops, and continuous professional development initiatives were incorporated throughout the project lifecycle to ensure that local stakeholders, including government officials and technical teams, could sustainably manage, maintain, and evolve the ICT infrastructure post-implementation. Additionally, the program proactively established dedicated maintenance funds to secure financial resources for ongoing system upkeep, upgrades, and troubleshooting, thereby addressing one of the critical challenges—funding gaps—that often jeopardize ICT project longevity in small island developing states.

Complementing the technical and financial measures, several Caribbean governments established dedicated ICT governance bodies tasked explicitly with the stewardship of digital assets and policies after project deployment. These governance organizations are mandated not only to oversee the technical operations but also to coordinate cross-sectoral integration of ICTs into broader development agendas. Their roles include policy formulation, resource allocation, regulatory compliance, and stakeholder engagement, which are fundamental to institutionalizing ICT sustainability. By embedding ICT responsibility within formal organizational frameworks, these bodies foster accountability, continuity, and adaptive management, helping to mitigate risks related to political changes or resource re-allocation that historically undermine project sustainability in the region.

At the regional level, cooperative efforts such as those spearheaded by the Eastern Caribbean Telecommunications Authority (ECTEL) illustrate the power of shared governance to enhance ICT project resilience and sustainability. ECTEL facilitates harmonization of policies, regulatory alignment, and coordinated infrastructure development among member states, leveraging collective bargaining power to achieve cost efficiencies and interoperability across island networks. ECTEL's initiatives include common standards for spectrum management, unified cybersecurity policies, and joint capacity building programs that transcend individual national limitations. This regional collaboration not only reduces duplication and fragmentation but also creates a scalable platform for continuous innovation and service expansion. Moreover, it provides a forum for knowledge exchange and mutual support, enabling member states to learn from each other's best practices and collectively surmount challenges linked to the Caribbean's unique geographic and socio-economic landscape.

These sustainability measures within CARCIP, national ICT governance structures, and regional frameworks like ECTEL demonstrate a layered and integrated approach essential for fostering long-term success in Caribbean ICT projects. By simultaneously addressing capacity development, financial provisioning, institutional ownership, and multilateral cooperation, these initiatives contribute to building resilient ICT ecosystems that support sustained social, economic, and technological progress. Their strategies also offer valuable lessons and models for other developing regions grappling with analogous challenges of ICT project sustainability in complex and resource-constrained environments.

Scaling Successful Initiatives across the Region

Why Scale Matters

Scaling successful ICT initiatives is essential for maximizing the benefits of digital projects and ensuring that their positive impacts reach a broader population beyond initial pilot implementations. For the Caribbean region, which is characterized by a collection of small island states sharing similar socio-economic profiles, scaling provides a unique opportunity to pool scarce resources, harmonize efforts, and leverage collective expertise. Rather than each island acting in isolation, regional scaling enables economies of scale, reduces duplication of effort, and promotes interoperability of systems. This can expedite access to ICT-enabled services such as e-government, e-health, e-learning, and digital business platforms, thereby accelerating regional socio-economic development. Effectively scaled initiatives also serve as powerful catalysts for fostering innovation ecosystems, enhancing competitiveness, and empowering citizens across multiple jurisdictions simultaneously.

Considerations for Scaling

Contextual Adaptation: Scaling does not imply mere replication. Each initiative must retain its core functional components while being carefully adapted to account for local cultural nuances, infrastructural realities, and regulatory or policy environments unique to each jurisdiction. For instance, bandwidth availability, digital literacy levels, and community needs may vary between islands and necessitate tailored implementation approaches. This ensures that scaled deployments are sensitive to users' contexts and therefore more likely to achieve sustained adoption and impact.

Interoperability and Standards: The foundation of scalable ICT initiatives lies in designing solutions based on open standards, interoperable protocols, and modular architectures. This approach facilitates seamless integration across heterogeneous systems and service providers prevalent in the Caribbean. It also supports future scalability by enabling incremental enhancements without full system replacements. Adherence to standards promotes vendor neutrality, reduces lock-in risks, and encourages innovation. Regional bodies such as the Caribbean Telecommunications Union (CTU) play a central role in advocating for standardization to foster compatibility and efficient service delivery across island networks.

Sustainable Business Models: For projects to scale effectively, they must be underpinned by sustainable and replicable business models. These models should clearly articulate revenue streams, cost recovery mechanisms, and financing approaches that accommodate scaling costs such as expanded infrastructure maintenance, customer support, and ongoing capacity building. Public funding alone is often insufficient; blending donor funds with user fees, private sector investments, and public-private partnerships (PPPs) can secure financial viability. Business models must also consider affordability for end-users to avoid excluding marginalized communities.

Strong Regional Coordination: Effective coordination across Caribbean states is paramount in orchestrating regional scaling efforts. Entities like CARICOM and the Eastern Caribbean Telecommunications Authority (ECTEL) serve as indispensable platforms for strategy alignment, policy harmonization, joint procurement, and shared technical resources. Their oversight and facilitation help reconcile national priorities with regional objectives, avoid fragmented approaches, and accelerate knowledge transfer. Strong coordination also ensures that regulatory environments are conducive to scaling and that stakeholders commit to collaborative frameworks sustaining initiatives long term.

Capacity and Knowledge Sharing: Scaling initiatives necessitate enhanced human and institutional capacities. Establishing regional centers of excellence focused on ICT innovation, management, and training fosters skill development and disseminates best practices. Similarly, creating communities of practice—including cross-island practitioner networks, academic partnerships, and user groups—stimulates ongoing learning and peer-to-peer support. These mechanisms prevent isolated siloes of knowledge and empower countries with limited expertise to benefit from pooled resources and experience. Capacity building also extends to equipping policymakers with the competencies needed to oversee complex scaled deployments.

Additional Strategic Considerations

The adoption of adaptive and iterative scaling methodologies is recommended to allow flexibility in responding to emerging challenges or shifts within island environments. Pilot phases can be embedded within scaling roadmaps to validate assumptions and fine-tune project designs. Moreover, scaling efforts should integrate robust monitoring and evaluation mechanisms tied to key performance indicators (KPIs) that measure both operational effectiveness and socio-economic outcomes across varied contexts. This data-driven approach allows continuous improvement and demonstrates scaling impact to funders and stakeholders.

Digital divide issues warrant proactive strategies within scaling frameworks, ensuring equitable access to advanced ICT services across urban, rural, and marginalized populations. This may require complementary infrastructure investments, targeted literacy programs, and culturally sensitive outreach campaigns. Furthermore, environmental sustainability considerations—such as energy-efficient technologies and disaster-resilient infrastructure—must be embedded into scaling plans given the vulnerability of Caribbean islands to climate change and natural events.

In Summary, scaling proven ICT initiatives throughout the Caribbean region magnifies their social and economic benefits and reinforces regional integration. Achieving this requires balancing fidelity to successful core solutions with local adaptability, underpinning deployments with interoperable standards and sustainable business models, fostering strong regional governance, and building shared capacities for knowledge and skills enhancement. By embracing these principles, Caribbean ICT projects can move beyond fragmented, pilot-level implementations towards resilient, scalable, and inclusive digital ecosystems that propel the region's development into the future.

Successful Examples of Scaled ICT Projects

E-Government Portals

In recent years, several Eastern Caribbean countries have successfully launched integrated e-government portals that unify the delivery of citizen-centric services across multiple government agencies. These portals, often inspired by regional best practices and collaborative frameworks, aim to streamline access to services such as tax filing, business registration, social service applications, and utility payments, all through a single, cohesive online platform. The scaling of these portals from pilot projects to fully operational systems across multiple jurisdictions has considerably improved government responsiveness, transparency, and efficiency. Notably, this regional scaling enables smaller states to share development costs, align security protocols, and ensure interoperability of systems, thereby reducing duplication and fostering cross-border electronic transactions. The successful integration of these portals has also encouraged increased citizen engagement, reducing the need for in-person visits and paperwork, and has set a foundation for more complex digital government ecosystems in the Caribbean.

E-Learning Platforms

The expansion of e-learning platforms stands as a testament to the power of regional collaboration in education technology among Caribbean countries. What began as pilot projects in select schools—often supported by regional education ministries and international donors—have now evolved into widespread, country-level deployments that provide students and educators with access to digital course materials, virtual classrooms, and remote assessment tools. This scaling has been facilitated by investments in broadband infrastructure and the adoption of cloud-based learning management systems tailored to regional curricula and multilingual contexts. Importantly, scaling efforts have integrated comprehensive teacher training programs, ensuring educators possess the digital literacy and instructional design skills necessary for effective technology use. The widespread adoption of e-learning platforms has enhanced educational equity by reaching students in remote and underserved areas, supporting continuous learning during natural disasters or public health crises, and fostering skills that align with 21st-century workforce needs. These initiatives represent a critical stride in the region's efforts to modernize education systems through technology.

Smart Agriculture Solutions

The Caribbean's agricultural sector has witnessed promising advancements via the regional scaling of smart agriculture ICT tools, initially piloted in local communities. Digital solutions such as mobile weather monitoring apps, pest and disease early warning systems, remote sensing technologies, and online market access platforms have been adapted and expanded to neighboring islands, addressing the unique challenges of small-scale farming across dispersed geographies. These technologies harness mobile telecommunications and Internet of Things (IoT) devices to provide real-time data that empowers farmers to optimize crop yields, manage risks associated with climate variability, and access fairer markets. Regional agricultural cooperatives and extension services have played an instrumental role in facilitating farmer training and promoting sustainable technology adoption. By sharing knowledge, best practices, and infrastructural resources, Caribbean countries have enhanced the resilience and productivity of their agricultural economies. This scaling of smart agriculture solutions contributes to food security, rural development, and climate adaptation efforts region-wide.

Challenges in Regional Scaling

The regional scaling of ICT initiatives across the Caribbean faces a number of complexes, interrelated challenges that reflect the unique socioeconomic, infrastructural, and governance landscapes of the island nations involved. These barriers impact the ability to replicate and expand successful pilot projects efficiently and sustainably, often requiring nuanced, adaptive approaches.

Differences in ICT Maturity and Infrastructure Capacity

One of the foremost challenges to regional scaling is the uneven ICT maturity levels and infrastructure readiness across the Caribbean islands. While some countries or territories may have relatively advanced broadband networks, data centers, and ICT policy frameworks, others may still be grappling with basic connectivity issues and nascent digital governance systems. This disparity creates an uneven playing field for scaling, where solutions optimized for one environment may falter or require substantial modification to function effectively elsewhere. For example, islands with limited submarine cable connectivity or insufficient power infrastructure face hurdles in deploying bandwidth-intensive services such as e-government portals or cloud-based education platforms. The variance in digital literacy and availability of skilled ICT professionals also influences adaptation speed and quality of local support, making capacity-building a critical and challenging requirement in scaling efforts.

Funding and Policy Misalignments

Scaling ICT projects beyond initial geographies requires sustained and harmonized funding models, yet many Caribbean countries suffer from fragmented or incompatible policy environments and financial planning.

National priorities vary, and without coherent regional coordination on budget allocations, cost-sharing, and financial sustainability strategies, projects risk stalling or losing momentum. Funding gaps can emerge when donor assistance concludes or when political shifts lead to re-prioritization at individual national levels. This lack of alignment complicates attempts to implement standardized solutions regionally and to develop unified financing instruments such as regional innovation funds or pooled procurement mechanisms. Disparate regulatory environments further exacerbate the challenge, as differing tax regimes, licensing requirements, and ICT regulations impose administrative burden and restrict market growth for ICT services spanning multiple countries.

Data Privacy Laws and Regulatory Harmonization Needs

As ICT solutions increasingly rely on cross-border data exchanges, cloud service deployments, and interoperable platforms, divergent data privacy and cybersecurity laws across Caribbean nations present a significant obstacle. Inconsistent legal frameworks concerning data protection, digital identities, and electronic transactions raise compliance complexities, risks of data breaches, and legal ambiguities that deter regional integration. The absence of a harmonized regional legal regime for digital governance limits the ability to deploy region-wide e-government services or shared digital health records efficiently. Caribbean policymakers and regulatory authorities face the ongoing task of crafting and mutually adopting standards that balance security, privacy, and innovation incentives, while addressing variations in institutional capacity and cultural attitudes toward privacy. Until greater alignment is achieved, these regulatory gaps create friction and delay in scaling efforts.

Variability in Political Will and Leadership

The varying degrees of political commitment, leadership stability, and institutional readiness across Caribbean nations represent a critical challenge in regional scaling. Leadership changes, governance disruptions, or lack of sustained vision for digital transformation can interrupt project progress or cause inconsistent implementation priorities. Political will directly influences resource allocation, public sector reforms, stakeholder engagement, and the willingness to embrace innovative ICT solutions. While some governments have demonstrated strong support through clear national ICT roadmaps and dedicated ministries, others struggle with diffuse responsibilities and fragmented mandates. Effective regional scaling requires synchronized political backing that transcends election cycles and administrative changes, fostering a shared regional agenda supported by consistent policy advocacy, cooperative agreements, and high-level champions.

By addressing these overarching challenges through context-aware strategies, enhanced regional cooperation, and adaptive governance models, Caribbean ICT scaling initiatives can better navigate the complexities intrinsic to a diverse archipelago. Building capacity while harmonizing policies, financing, and leadership commitments is essential to transforming isolated pilots into sustainable, regionally integrated digital services that deliver inclusive benefits.

Strategies to Foster Regional Scaling

Establish Regional ICT Strategic Frameworks that Outline Priorities and Roles

A crucial foundational step in fostering successful regional scaling of ICT initiatives is the development of clear, comprehensive strategic frameworks at the regional level. These frameworks not only articulate shared priorities and goals aligned with Caribbean development agendas but also define the roles and responsibilities of participating countries, regional organizations, and stakeholders. By setting common targets—such as regional broadband access, e-government interoperability, or digital literacy benchmarks—countries enhance alignment and reduce strategic fragmentation. Frameworks should integrate mechanisms for monitoring and evaluation, allowing iterative refinement to respond to emerging regional challenges. Successful frameworks foster shared ownership and guide harmonized efforts in infrastructure development, policy harmonization, capacity building, and financing models. The involvement of regional bodies such as CARICOM, the Caribbean Telecommunications Union (CTU), and the Eastern Caribbean Telecommunications Authority (ECTEL) ensures legitimacy, coordination, and resource mobilization for implementing these frameworks.

Develop Joint Funding Mechanisms Including Pooled Donor Resources

Securing sustainable financing for scaling ICT projects across multiple Caribbean jurisdictions requires innovative funding strategies that transcend individual country budgets. Establishing joint funding mechanisms, including pooled donor resources, can create more robust and predictable financial support for regional initiatives. This may take the form of regional ICT development funds, co-financing arrangements, or blended finance models combining public sector funds with private investments and donor grants. Pooling funds not only increases the scale and scope of ICT projects but also attracts larger development partners and investment. Such mechanisms encourage efficiency by enabling bulk procurement of technology and services, reducing costs, and facilitating risk sharing. Transparent governance structures for fund management that promote accountability and equitable allocation of resources are essential to maintain donor confidence and regional stakeholder trust.

Promote Cross-Country Training and Staff Exchanges to Build Capacity

Scaling ICT projects regionally demands not only technological infrastructure but also significant human capacity development. Promoting cross-country training programs and staff exchanges allows Caribbean nations to bridge capability gaps, share expertise, and accelerate learning curves. Regional training academies or centers of excellence can deliver standardized curricula covering project management, ICT governance, cybersecurity, cloud technologies, and emerging digital skills. Facilitating personnel exchanges enables the transfer of tacit knowledge and strengthens institutional ties, which are vital for collaborative ICT maintenance and innovation. This strategy also develops a resilient talent pool dispersed across countries, mitigating challenges posed by brain drain and localized skill shortages. Collaborative professional networks and communities of practice foster ongoing dialogue and problem-solving among ICT practitioners in the Caribbean.

Ensure Inclusive Stakeholder Involvement from the Outset

Early and sustained involvement of diverse stakeholders—including government agencies, private sector partners, civil society groups, end-users, and regional bodies—is critical for the success of scaled ICT initiatives. Inclusive engagement promotes broader ownership, improves solution relevance, and fosters social acceptance, vital for long-term sustainability. Stakeholders' input should inform the design, deployment, and governance of regional ICT projects to ensure alignment with local needs and cultural contexts. Participatory approaches help identify and mitigate risks such as resistance to change or digital exclusion. Transparent communication, multi-stakeholder steering committees, and regular forums for feedback encourage trust, cooperation, and collective problem solving, enhancing the likelihood of project success and stable scaling.

Use Technology-Neutral Platforms Adaptable to Diverse Contexts

Employing technology-neutral platforms is a strategic choice for scaling ICT initiatives effectively across a region marked by diverse technical capacities and infrastructure environments. Solutions based on open standards and interoperable architectures can be more easily customized to accommodate varied local conditions, such as differences in internet bandwidth, legacy systems, regulatory environments, and user capabilities. Technology neutrality avoids vendor lock-in and promotes flexibility in integrating emerging tools and services. Platforms that are modular and scalable facilitate incremental deployments and phased upgrades, minimizing upfront costs and operational risks. This approach enables Caribbean countries to leverage shared infrastructure while tailoring service delivery to country-specific contexts, thereby maximizing impact and adoption.

Additional Recommendations

Establish Regional Governance Structures: Strong oversight bodies that coordinate policy, technical standards, funding, and implementation across islands help institutionalize scaling efforts and prevent fragmentation.

Leverage Regional Innovation Hubs: Promote innovation ecosystems that fund and support local ICT startups and digital entrepreneurs' region-wide to stimulate sustainable economic growth.

Facilitate Legal and Regulatory Harmonization: Regional agreements to align digital policies, privacy laws, and cybersecurity protocols reduce barriers to cross-border ICT service delivery.

Encourage Data Sharing and Integration: Secure and privacy-compliant sharing of regional data sets enhances e-government and disaster resilience capabilities.

By adopting and tailoring these strategies, Caribbean ICT projects can overcome the critical hurdles of fragmentation, resource scarcity, and capacity constraints, driving inclusive and lasting digital transformation across the region.

Conclusion

Measuring impact and ensuring the sustainability of ICT projects constitute fundamental pillars of effective digital development strategies within the Caribbean region. The establishment of clear, relevant, and actionable key performance indicators (KPIs) is essential for project leaders and stakeholders. These KPIs enable ongoing monitoring, performance evaluation, and timely adaptation of strategies to evolving environmental, technological, and social conditions. Through systematic measurement, projects can not only demonstrate accountability but also identify areas requiring intervention, thereby enhancing the likelihood of successful outcomes.

Embedding sustainability in ICT projects demands taking a holistic approach encompassing technical resilience, financial soundness, institutional capacity, and social inclusion. Technical sustainability ensures systems remain scalable, interoperable, secure, and maintainable in the face of rapid technological change and environmental risks unique to Caribbean Island states, such as hurricanes and climate variability. Financial sustainability requires thoughtful planning beyond initial funding, incorporating diverse and resilient revenue models, cost recovery mechanisms, and public-private partnerships to secure operational continuity. Institutional sustainability hinges on building local expertise through capacity development, strengthening governance frameworks, and fostering leadership committed to digital transformation. Social sustainability involves engaging communities and users meaningfully to ensure ICT solutions reflect local needs, cultural preferences, and bridge digital divides—especially for marginalized and rural populations.

Finally, scaling successful ICT initiatives regionally across the Caribbean is critical to amplifying their socio-economic impact and fostering regional integration. Scaling facilitates resource pooling, shared expertise, harmonized policies, and service interoperability, which are pragmatic responses to the region's many small island states with shared development challenges and opportunities. Effective regional scaling drives inclusive growth, enhances access to governance, education, health, and economic services, and builds collective resilience in a dynamic global digital landscape.

By conscientiously adopting these approaches, IT project managers and policymakers in the Caribbean are positioned to transition from fragmented, pilot-stage experiments to lasting, integrated ICT ecosystems. Such ecosystems can uplift communities, invigorate public and private sectors, and accelerate the region's path toward a more connected, equitable, and prosperous digital future.

Chapter 9

The Future of ICT in the Eastern Caribbean — Emerging Trends

Blockchain: Building Trust and Financial Inclusion

Blockchain technology is rapidly emerging as a transformative tool with vast potential to foster financial inclusion, enhance transparency, and build trust across global economies. This is particularly significant in regions like the Eastern Caribbean, where a collection of small island states faces unique systemic challenges such as limited financial infrastructure, heavy reliance on traditional and often inaccessible banking systems, and heightened vulnerability to corruption, inefficiencies, and economic disruptions. By leveraging blockchain technology, these nations can overcome some of their most pressing economic and social limitations, unlocking new pathways for inclusive growth and sustainable development.

The Eastern Caribbean Central Bank (ECCB) has taken pioneering and ambitious steps towards this future by launching the DCash initiative, the world's first blockchain-based digital currency deployed across a multi-state currency union. This landmark project not only showcases regional innovation but also positions the Eastern Caribbean Currency Union (ECCU) as a global leader in the research, development, and practical application of central bank digital currencies (CBDCs). DCash is engineered to empower citizens who have been traditionally underserved by banks—those without bank accounts or easy access to financial services. By integrating these populations into the digital economy, DCash reduces barriers to financial access and inclusion, enabling safer, faster, and more cost-effective transactions across national borders within the region. This is a critical step towards democratizing access to financial tools that support everyday livelihoods, business activities, and government service delivery.

Beyond the domain of financial services, blockchain's potential applications extend comprehensively into various essential government functions—further catalyzing efficiency, transparency, and accountability. Governments in the Eastern Caribbean can harness blockchain-based distributed ledger technology to revolutionize the management of land registries, which traditionally suffer from inefficiencies, inaccurate records, and fraud. Similarly, health information systems and citizen identity verification processes can be secured and streamlined by leveraging immutable blockchain records, enhancing privacy and reducing bureaucratic delays. Public procurement, often beset by corruption and inefficiency, can benefit immensely from transparent and tamper-proof blockchain frameworks that make transactions traceable and auditable in real-time. These applications collectively contribute to strengthening governance, improving public trust, and creating an environment that deters corrupt practices.

For entrepreneurs and small business owners, blockchain-based innovations such as smart contracts provide a powerful mechanism to facilitate cross-border commerce without relying on costly intermediaries or prolonged settlement times. Smart contracts—self-executing agreements with the terms of the contract directly written into code—can automate payments, enforce contract terms, and reduce the risks associated with international trade. This can stimulate trade, attract foreign investment, and support the growth of small and medium-sized enterprises (SMEs) that are the backbone of many Eastern Caribbean economies.

Despite these promising developments, the Eastern Caribbean still faces several significant hurdles that threaten to slow blockchain adoption and limit its benefits. Regulatory uncertainty is a key challenge, as governments grapple with how to create frameworks that encourage innovation while protecting consumers and ensuring financial stability. There is also a notable gap in technical expertise; the specialized skills required to build, deploy, and maintain blockchain systems are scarce in the region, necessitating substantial investment in education and capacity-building programs. Moreover, heightened digital dependency introduces a range of cybersecurity risks, requiring robust and continuously updated defense mechanisms to protect sensitive data and digital assets from cyber threats.

To fully realize the transformative potential of blockchain technology, coordinated efforts by governments, financial regulators, educational institutions, and the private sector are essential. This includes enacting clear enabling legislation that fosters innovation while providing regulatory certainty, implementing comprehensive skills development and training programs to build a knowledgeable workforce, and establishing resilient cybersecurity strategies and infrastructure to safeguard users and systems. By addressing these challenges proactively, the Eastern Caribbean can harness blockchain not only to advance financial inclusion and good governance but also to drive economic diversification, resilience, and sustainable development for the entire region.

In summary, blockchain offers the Eastern Caribbean an unprecedented opportunity to leapfrog traditional constraints, innovate at scale, and drive a more inclusive and transparent future. With strategic investments, forward-thinking policies, and collaborative partnerships, the region is well-positioned to become a global exemplar of blockchain-enabled digital transformation.

Quantum Computing: The Next Computational Leap

Quantum computing remains in its early developmental stages, yet its potential to revolutionize many facets of science, technology, and industry is undeniable. Unlike classical computers, which process data in binary bits—representing either a 0 or a 1—quantum computers operate using quantum bits, or qubits. These qubits exploit principles of quantum mechanics such as superposition and entanglement, enabling them to perform complex calculations at speeds exponentially faster than classical machines. This capability promises to unlock solutions to currently intractable problems in fields ranging from cryptography and logistics optimization to climate modeling and drug discovery.

For the Eastern Caribbean, the strategic importance of quantum computing lies primarily in its long-term potential to address pressing regional challenges, particularly those related to climate vulnerability. The small island states in this region are disproportionately exposed to the adverse effects of climate change, including more frequent and intense hurricanes, rising sea levels, and coastal erosion. These environmental threats jeopardize livelihoods, ecosystems, infrastructure, and economic stability. Quantum-powered simulations and modeling could dramatically enhance the precision and reliability of climate forecasts and disaster risk assessments. By processing massive amounts of environmental data with unparalleled speed and sophistication, quantum technologies could enable governments, disaster management agencies, and planners to develop optimized evacuation strategies, allocate emergency resources more efficiently, and design resilient infrastructure tailored to withstand future climate shocks. This improved predictive capacity would be transformative in safeguarding lives and sustaining development.

In the financial and cybersecurity spheres, the dual-edged nature of quantum computing is especially important for the Eastern Caribbean. On the one hand, quantum computers hold the potential to undermine traditional encryption algorithms currently safeguarding sensitive government, business, and citizen data. Many classical cryptographic systems—such as RSA and ECC—could be rendered obsolete by sufficiently powerful quantum attacks, exposing digital infrastructure to significant security risks. This looming threat necessitates urgent proactive measures: the region must begin transitioning toward quantum-resistant cryptographic techniques designed to withstand quantum decryption capabilities. On the other hand, quantum computing also offers powerful new tools to enhance cybersecurity defenses, enabling the development of secure quantum communication channels and advanced detection of cyber threats. Building expertise in these technologies will be critical to protecting digital ecosystems in an increasingly interconnected world.

Direct investment in the sophisticated hardware and infrastructure required for quantum computing may appear prohibitively expensive for the Eastern Caribbean's small economies in the near term. However, the regional approach does not need to rely exclusively on domestic quantum hardware development. Instead, universities, research institutions, and policymakers in the Eastern Caribbean can strategically prioritize establishing knowledge partnerships and collaborative research initiatives with global quantum leaders—such as academic institutions, technology companies, and multilateral organizations active in quantum research. Early engagement in international networks can provide critical access to cutting-edge developments, training opportunities, and talent pipelines. This collaborative stance will also help the region shape its own quantum strategy and capitalize on potential spin-offs for local industries without bearing the full cost of infrastructure.

By proactively building human capital through specialized education programs, investing in quantum literacy, and fostering innovation ecosystems that encourage cross-disciplinary collaboration, the Eastern Caribbean can position itself to benefit from the coming quantum revolution. Early preparation will help avoid digital marginalization and ensure that this region is not left behind as the world transitions to fundamentally new computational paradigms.

In conclusion, while quantum computing currently remains in its nascent phase, its long-term transformative potential cannot be underestimated—particularly for climate resilience, security, and economic competitiveness in the Eastern Caribbean. Through strategic foresight, targeted partnerships, and sustained investments in knowledge development, the region can harness quantum technologies to become more resilient, secure, and innovative in the decades ahead. This forward-looking stance will be essential for navigating the complexities of a rapidly evolving technological landscape and ensuring sustainable development for future generations.

Brain-Computer Interfaces (BCIs): Bridging Mind and Machine

Brain-computer interfaces (BCIs), once the realm of science fiction, are rapidly evolving into practical technologies with a wide range of research and commercial applications. Pioneering companies such as Neuralink and OpenBCI, alongside numerous academic consortia worldwide, are making significant strides in developing systems that enable direct communication between the human brain and digital devices. These advances open up transformative possibilities across healthcare, education, and beyond, offering novel solutions to longstanding challenges.

For the Eastern Caribbean, BCIs present a particularly promising opportunity to revolutionize healthcare delivery, especially given the region's limited availability of specialized medical personnel and infrastructure. BCIs can serve as powerful assistive technologies for persons with disabilities, including those living with paralysis, stroke survivors, or individuals suffering from neurodegenerative diseases such as Parkinson's or Alzheimer's. By enabling direct neural control over prosthetic devices or communication aids, BCIs can significantly improve the quality of life and independence for these populations. Furthermore, integrated with telemedicine platforms, BCIs could facilitate remote rehabilitation and continuous neurological monitoring, reducing the need for frequent travel to specialized centers that are often centralized and difficult to access across the dispersed island states. Such capabilities would not only broaden access to critical care but also optimize resource allocation within already strained healthcare systems.

Education represents another frontier where BCIs could have a transformative impact in the Eastern Caribbean.

Given regional challenges such as limited teacher-to-student ratios, disparities in educational resources across islands, and infrastructural constraints, BCIs offer innovative ways to personalize learning experiences. By monitoring real-time neural indicators of cognitive engagement, attention, and mental fatigue, BCI systems could help educators dynamically adapt content delivery to meet the unique learning needs of each student. This could enable more effective and efficient instruction, fostering deeper understanding and retention of knowledge. Additionally, BCI-driven adaptive learning tools could support students with special educational needs and enhance remote learning platforms, helping to bridge gaps in education quality and accessibility across diverse communities in the region.

However, as with any emerging technology that interfaces intimately with human biology, BCIs raise profound ethical, cultural, and privacy considerations that require careful deliberation. Caribbean societies may have varying perspectives on the acceptability and implications of direct brain-data collection, which raises questions about individual consent, data ownership, and the potential misuse of neural information. Who holds the rights to the sensitive neural data captured through BCIs? How will privacy be protected against unauthorized access or exploitation? What safeguards will be put in place to prevent discrimination or coercion based on neural data? Addressing these complex issues necessitates the development of comprehensive policies and regulatory frameworks that reflect regional values and cultural contexts while aligning with global ethical standards. These frameworks should aim to ensure that BCIs are deployed in ways that enhance human potential, dignity, and autonomy without infringing on fundamental rights.

Moreover, public awareness campaigns and community engagement initiatives will be essential to educate citizens on the benefits, risks, and responsible use of BCI technology. Building trust and transparency around these emerging tools will facilitate broader acceptance and guide socially responsible innovation.

In summary, brain-computer interfaces hold tremendous promise to transform healthcare and education in the Eastern Caribbean by overcoming resource limitations and enabling highly personalized support for vulnerable populations. Yet, realizing this potential requires a balanced approach that combines technological innovation with robust ethical governance, informed public dialogue, and regional collaboration. By proactively addressing the technical, social, and regulatory challenges, the Eastern Caribbean can position itself at the forefront of integrating BCIs in ways that empower individuals and strengthen communities, shaping a future where human potential is expanded thoughtfully, inclusively, and responsibly.

Generative AI (GenAI): Automating Creativity and Innovation

Generative artificial intelligence (AI) has already begun to revolutionize industries globally by enabling the rapid automation of content creation across a diverse range of media, including text, images, music, and software development. This technological advancement represents a profound shift in how creative processes are conducted, unlocking unprecedented opportunities for innovation, efficiency, and scale. For the Eastern Caribbean, generative AI has the potential to be a true game-changer, especially for the region's burgeoning creative economies, small businesses, and tourism sectors.

One of the most promising applications of generative AI in the Eastern Caribbean lies in enhancing tourism marketing and experiences, which are critical pillars of economic activity for many island states. AI-powered tools can generate immersive and personalized virtual tourism experiences that allow potential visitors to explore destinations digitally before travel. Such experiences could include interactive 3D tours of iconic landmarks, culturally rich storytelling through AI-generated video and audio content, and customized marketing campaigns tailored to individual preferences and travel histories. These innovations can significantly boost visitor engagement, increase tourist arrivals, and extend the reach of local cultural heritage globally. Moreover, generative AI can help small hospitality businesses and tour operators create professional-grade branding, promotional materials, and customer outreach automatically, reducing operational costs and enabling them to compete more effectively on an international stage without the need for large marketing teams.

Beyond tourism, generative AI offers substantial benefits to small businesses and startups across various sectors in the Eastern Caribbean. By leveraging AI tools, entrepreneurs

306

can automate routine tasks such as content creation, customer service, and product design, thereby freeing up resources to focus on strategic growth and innovation. For instance, AI can assist in generating marketing copy, designing logos, composing music for advertisements, or even developing initial software prototypes. This democratization of advanced creative capabilities empowers businesses to scale rapidly and enter global markets with competitive offerings, fostering economic diversification and job creation within the region.

Education and workforce development can also be transformed by generative AI technologies. These systems can deliver highly customized learning experiences by tailoring curriculum, pace, and style according to individual student needs and preferences. This personalized approach can help address challenges such as uneven educational resources, varied literacy levels, and limited access to specialized instruction across the islands. For professionals, AI-driven platforms can facilitate continuous upskilling and reskilling by generating targeted training materials that adapt dynamically to evolving industry demands. Such capabilities will be crucial in preparing the Eastern Caribbean's workforce for the increasing digitization and automation of the global economy.

In the realm of governance and public policy, generative AI can serve as a powerful decision-support tool. Policymakers can use AI models and simulations to visualize complex economic scenarios, forecast social and environmental trends, and test the potential impacts of policy choices before implementation. By doing so, governments can adopt more evidence-based and proactive approaches to addressing challenges such as climate change, economic inequality, and public health crises. This data-driven governance model can enhance the responsiveness, transparency, and effectiveness of government institutions.

Despite these exciting possibilities, the adoption of generative AI in the Eastern Caribbean is not without significant challenges. One major concern is the risk of misinformation and disinformation, as AI-generated content can be convincingly realistic yet misleading or false, potentially undermining public trust and social cohesion. Intellectual property rights present another complex issue, as the boundaries around ownership and authorship of AI-created works are still being defined globally. Furthermore, the widespread use of generative AI demands a high level of digital literacy so that citizens can critically evaluate the authenticity and source of digital content. Without sufficient understanding and awareness, there is a risk that communities could become vulnerable to manipulation or economic displacement.

To harness the full benefits of generative AI while mitigating associated risks, strategic investments must be made in comprehensive digital literacy programs, skills training, and robust regulatory frameworks. Governments, educational institutions, and the private sector need to collaborate to establish clear guidelines on ethical AI use, data privacy, and intellectual property protections tailored to regional realities. Encouraging innovation ecosystems that support startups and creative entrepreneurs in adopting and developing AI technologies will also be key to positioning the Eastern Caribbean as a vibrant hub for digital creativity and technological innovation.

In conclusion, generative AI holds transformative potential for the Eastern Caribbean by catalyzing growth in tourism, empowering small businesses, personalizing education, and enhancing governance. With deliberate planning, capacity building, and governance, the region can maximize these opportunities to drive sustainable economic development, foster resilience, and elevate its global competitiveness in the digital age.

Large Language Models (LLMs): Powering the Next Digital Wave

Large Language Models (LLMs), exemplified by systems such as ChatGPT and other GPT-based platforms, stand out as some of the most prominent and widely recognized applications of artificial intelligence today. These models excel in natural language processing (NLP), enabling complex capabilities including language translation, content summarization, information retrieval, and the facilitation of conversational interfaces at unprecedented scale and sophistication. Their capacity to understand and generate human-like text opens up numerous opportunities for education, governance, business, and cultural expression.

In the Eastern Caribbean, a region characterized by rich multilingualism—primarily English, French Creole, and Spanish—combined with disparities and limitations in educational resources, LLMs have the potential to significantly democratize access to knowledge and information. For students across these islands, AI-powered tutoring systems can provide personalized, on-demand academic support in multiple languages, helping to bridge learning gaps that traditional classroom settings sometimes struggle to address. These AI tutors can adapt to individual learning styles and pace, offer detailed explanations, and provide practice exercises, thus enhancing educational equity and facilitating lifelong learning.

Governments in the Eastern Caribbean can also harness LLM technology to transform public service delivery. By deploying AI chatbots via websites, mobile apps, and social media, governments can provide citizens with timely and accessible information on crucial topics such as healthcare advice, agricultural best practices, social services, and tourism. For example, rural farmers could receive AI-generated guidance on crop management or weather conditions in their preferred language, while tourists could interact with virtual assistants that cater to their language preference, improving overall experience and engagement. These improvements in service accessibility could have a particularly profound impact in remote or underserved communities, where access to human experts may be limited.

Moreover, LLMs offer significant promise for supporting the region's local media outlets and creative industries. Journalists, writers, and artists can utilize these tools to generate culturally relevant and linguistically appropriate content that resonates with diverse Caribbean audiences.

From drafting news stories and generating promotional material to scripting radio segments and composing poetry, AI can augment creative capacities and help scale content production without compromising cultural authenticity. However, this potential is tempered by critical concerns related to cultural preservation.

A notable risk associated with reliance on LLMs developed primarily using datasets from foreign sources is the inadvertent reinforcement of cultural homogenization. When AI systems predominantly represent perspectives shaped by dominant global narratives—often Western or Anglophone-centered—they may lack sensitivity to regional dialects, idiomatic expressions, historical contexts, and indigenous knowledge embedded in Caribbean identities. This can lead to the erosion of linguistic uniqueness and undermine cultural diversity, which are central to the Caribbean's rich heritage.

To prevent such outcomes, regional leaders, policymakers, and the AI research community must prioritize the curation and development of Caribbean-centered datasets for training and fine-tuning LLMs. This includes collecting, digitizing, and annotating texts that reflect local languages, oral histories, folklore, socio-political narratives, and cultural nuances. Collaborations between governments, universities, cultural institutions, and technology stakeholders will be crucial to building these datasets in an ethical, inclusive, and sustainable manner. In turn, AI tools trained on such contextual data can better represent and validate Caribbean lived experiences, fostering AI applications that truly empower local users and respect their identities.

Furthermore, capacity-building efforts are essential to develop local expertise in AI development, natural language processing, and data governance. By investing in education and research that focus on Caribbean linguistic and cultural contexts, the region can cultivate talent capable of leading in responsible AI innovation tailored to its distinct needs and values.

In conclusion, large language models offer transformative opportunities for the Eastern Caribbean to enhance education, public service, media, and cultural expression in ways that address regional multilingualism and resource constraints. However, realizing this potential fully and ethically requires intentional investment in Caribbean-centric datasets, the promotion of digital literacy, and the cultivation of local AI expertise. Such a comprehensive approach will enable the region to harness LLM technology as a powerful enabler of inclusive knowledge access, cultural preservation, and sustainable development in a rapidly evolving digital world.

Preparing for the Next Wave of Digital Transformation

To fully seize the transformative opportunities presented by emerging technologies such as blockchain, quantum computing, brain-computer interfaces, generative AI, and large language models, the Eastern Caribbean must undertake a comprehensive and systematic approach to digital preparedness. Central to this effort is a robust investment in digital literacy across all educational levels. From primary schools to tertiary institutions and adult learning programs, building a foundational understanding of digital skills is essential. This not only empowers individuals to harness new technologies effectively but also fosters an innovation mindset critical for the region's socio-economic development. Equipping students, teachers, public servants, and entrepreneurs with the ability to navigate, evaluate, and utilize digital tools will create a more inclusive digital ecosystem where benefits can be broadly shared.

Equally important is the expansion and modernization of digital infrastructure. Reliable, high-speed internet access is a prerequisite for leveraging cutting-edge technologies. The region must prioritize increasing broadband coverage and accelerating the rollout of advanced connectivity solutions such as 5G networks, especially in rural and remote areas that have historically been underserved. This infrastructure expansion ensures that all communities can participate in the digital economy, access remote education and healthcare services, and engage with government platforms seamlessly. Without widespread and affordable connectivity, technological innovation risks remaining concentrated in urban centers, exacerbating existing disparities.

In parallel with infrastructure growth, the Eastern Caribbean needs to adopt robust cybersecurity frameworks that are capable of addressing the evolving risks introduced by emerging technologies. As blockchain networks expand

and quantum computing capabilities develop, new vulnerabilities and attack vectors will emerge, requiring proactive risk mitigation strategies. Strengthening cybersecurity is essential to protect sensitive data, maintain public trust, and secure critical national digital assets against cyber threats, fraud, and misuse. Establishing regional cooperation on cybersecurity standards, threat intelligence sharing, and incident response will amplify resilience across island states.

Policy and regulatory readiness constitute another crucial pillar in this digital transformation journey. Governments must craft and implement forward-looking legal frameworks that govern the ethical and responsible use of artificial intelligence, ensure rigorous data privacy protections, and provide clarity around the use of digital currencies such as CBDCs. These regulations need to balance fostering innovation with safeguarding individual rights and financial stability. Furthermore, multi-stakeholder consultations will be vital in creating policies that reflect the region's unique socio-economic realities and cultural values, avoiding a one-size-fits-all approach often imported from other jurisdictions.

Talent development must also be a strategic priority. Encouraging the pursuit of science, technology, engineering, and mathematics (STEM) education from an early age will cultivate the next generation of skilled professionals capable of driving the region's technological future. Beyond education, mechanisms to retain this talent within the Eastern Caribbean must be implemented, addressing challenges such as brain drain through competitive job opportunities, research funding, and innovation incubation spaces. Empowering local innovators and entrepreneurs fosters an internal capacity to adapt, develop, and commercialize technologies tailored to regional needs.

Amid these positive advancements, it is critical to recognize that the digital divide remains a pressing concern. Without deliberate and inclusive policy measures, the rapid proliferation of advanced information and communication technologies risks deepening social and economic inequalities. Vulnerable groups—such as rural populations, low-income households, persons with disabilities, and marginalized communities—may face systemic barriers to accessing and benefiting from these technological gains. Bridging this divide requires targeted interventions that prioritize affordability, accessibility, digital education, and support services. Only through inclusive approaches can the Eastern Caribbean ensure that technological progress uplifts the entire population rather than leaving segments behind.

In conclusion, the Eastern Caribbean's ability to harness the full potential of emerging digital technologies hinges on a holistic strategy encompassing digital literacy, infrastructure development, cybersecurity, policy and regulation, and talent cultivation. By addressing these interconnected priorities with foresight and collaboration, the region can build a resilient, equitable, and forward-looking digital ecosystem that drives sustainable economic growth and societal wellbeing for all its citizens.

Regional Collaboration and Knowledge Sharing

Given the relatively small size and resource constraints faced by individual Eastern Caribbean states, no single country can effectively drive the region's digital transformation and technological transitions in isolation. The scope and scale of emerging technologies such as blockchain, quantum computing, advanced AI, and digital infrastructure investment require collaborative approaches that maximize regional strengths while mitigating individual limitations. In this context, regional cooperation through established bodies like the Organization of Eastern Caribbean States (OECS) is not only beneficial but essential. By working together, member states can pool financial resources, technical expertise, and institutional capacity to create shared platforms of innovation and development that would be prohibitively expensive or inefficient to build independently.

A critical area for regional collaboration is the establishment of shared research laboratories, innovation hubs, and regional data centers. Such joint infrastructure would significantly reduce costs by eliminating duplication and promoting economies of scale. More importantly, these centers would act as focal points for scientific research, technological experimentation, and startup incubation across the Eastern Caribbean. Innovation hubs could accelerate the development of homegrown solutions tailored to the region's unique economic, social, and environmental contexts, fostering greater technological self-reliance and resilience. Regional data centers, equipped with robust cybersecurity measures, would safeguard critical information assets and enable secure data sharing and analytics, facilitating smarter policymaking and business decision-making.

Beyond physical infrastructure, the creation and strengthening of knowledge-sharing networks will be pivotal for the Eastern Caribbean to keep pace with global technological advancements. Universities, research institutions, and technical colleges across the region can collaborate with international think tanks, leading academic centers, and private-sector innovators to exchange ideas, conduct joint research, and access cutting-edge resources. These partnerships provide an invaluable pipeline for talent development, capacity building, and access to emerging best practices. By fostering an ecosystem of continuous learning and innovation, the region can effectively "leapfrog" certain phases of traditional technological development, accelerating adoption and application in ways that maximize impact.

Pooling resources and collaborative knowledge generation also amplifies the Eastern Caribbean's influence in international digital and ICT governance arenas. These global discussions increasingly shape standards around data privacy, AI ethics, cross-border digital trade, cybersecurity, and telecommunications regulations—domains critical to the region's digital future. By presenting a unified regional voice, Eastern Caribbean states can assert their interests more effectively, advocate for policies that reflect their development priorities, and form strategic alliances that protect their unique cultural and economic identities.

In summary, the pathway to digital transformation in the Eastern Caribbean hinges on deepened regional cooperation that transcends individual national boundaries. Through shared investments in research and innovation infrastructure, the cultivation of dynamic knowledge networks, and coordinated engagement in global governance forums, the OECS and its member states can collectively build a robust, resilient, and inclusive digital ecosystem. This collaborative model not only optimizes scarce resources but also positions the region to harness technological advances as engines of sustainable economic growth, social equity, and regional integration in an increasingly interconnected world.

Insights from Global Thought Leaders

Thought leaders like Klaus Schwab (World Economic Prominent leaders in technology and innovation, including figures such as Klaus Schwab of the World Economic Forum, Satya Nadella of Microsoft, and Demis Hassabis of DeepMind, increasingly emphasize that the forthcoming wave of information and communication technologies (ICT) is not solely about technical breakthroughs. Rather, it is fundamentally about the responsible and thoughtful integration of these technologies into society. This shift underscores the importance of aligning technology with human values, ethical considerations, and long-term societal benefits—not merely advancing capabilities for their own sake.

For small island nations like those in the Eastern Caribbean, this perspective raises vital questions about how best to leverage emerging digital tools to foster resilience, sustainability, and cultural preservation. Given their geographic vulnerability to climate change, economic fragility, and rich diversity of cultural heritage, these nations face unique challenges that technology must address sensitively and inclusively. The adoption of ICT must be framed not only in terms of efficiency or growth but also as a means to improve the well-being of communities, safeguard traditions, and promote democratic participation.

In this context, the Eastern Caribbean is well-positioned to take a leadership role by championing human-centered design principles in its approach to ICT adoption. Human-centered design prioritizes the needs, values, and aspirations of people throughout the innovation process, ensuring that technology serves to enhance quality of life rather than disrupt social cohesion or diminish identity. By embedding these principles, the region can develop digital solutions that preserve local languages, celebrate cultural narratives, and support community-led development initiatives. This approach also involves transparent governance, inclusive decision-making, and ethical frameworks that protect user privacy and promote equitable access.

More broadly, the global South—including the Caribbean—has increasingly begun to influence and reshape narratives around digital innovation. These perspectives often depart from dominant Western-centric models by emphasizing community resilience, environmental stewardship, and creative expression as central to technological progress. The Caribbean, with its distinct historical experiences, diverse cultures, and strong communal ties, can make invaluable contributions to these evolving conversations. By articulating alternative models that prioritize sustainability and creativity, the region can provide a blueprint for responsible technology deployment that challenges conventional development paradigms.

Furthermore, by integrating ICT with cultural preservation and sustainable development goals, the Eastern Caribbean can inspire innovative solutions that address global challenges such as climate adaptation, social inclusion, and economic diversification. For instance, digital platforms can be used to document and disseminate intangible cultural heritage, while smart environmental monitoring systems can support disaster preparedness and resource management. These initiatives enhance regional resilience while showcasing how technology and culture can coexist in mutually reinforcing ways.

In sum, the Eastern Caribbean's future in the ICT landscape is not simply about adopting the latest technologies but about embedding these tools within a framework that values human dignity, cultural identity, and democratic participation. By leading with human-centered and community-grounded approaches, the region can contribute a powerful and unique voice to the global dialogue on digital innovation—one that champions sustainability, inclusivity, and creativity as cornerstones for building resilient societies in the digital age.

Chapter 10

Conclusion — Charting the Path Forward

Key Takeaways and Actionable Recommendations

The journey of integrating information and communication technologies (ICT) in the Eastern Caribbean has been both inspiring and sobering, reflecting a complex balance of achievements and challenges. Considerable progress has been made in expanding digital infrastructure, developing e-services, and fostering regional cooperation among small island states. These advancements have laid important groundwork for digital transformation. However, the findings from recent research and project assessments underscore that many ICT initiatives continue to falter due to issues such as inadequate planning, fragmented governance structures, and insufficient levels of user adoption. This mixed experience highlights the need for more strategic, coordinated, and inclusive approaches moving forward.

Several key lessons emerge from the review of ICT projects and strategies across the region. First and foremost, holistic planning is absolutely essential. ICT initiatives cannot be approached purely as technical add-ons or isolated interventions; rather, they must be carefully integrated into broader national development frameworks.

321

This includes alignment with educational reforms to build human capital, policies that enhance private-sector competitiveness, and social development goals. Projects that fail to connect with the wider socio-economic context often struggle to achieve meaningful impact or sustainability. Effective ICT integration requires that technology be viewed as an enabler within a comprehensive developmental vision instead of an end in itself.

Second, securing broad stakeholder buy-in is a critical determinant of success. Without genuine support and engagement from a wide array of actors—including communities, business leaders, civil society, and political decision-makers—even the most well-financed and technologically advanced projects are at risk of failure. Ensuring that the needs, priorities, and concerns of different stakeholders are addressed builds ownership and trust, which are crucial for sustained use and scalability. Participatory approaches to project design, implementation, and evaluation therefore must become integral components of ICT strategies.

Third, capacity-building remains a persistent bottleneck across the region. Despite growing investments, significant skills gaps persist in areas such as cybersecurity, artificial intelligence, project management, and other advanced ICT domains. These gaps limit the ability of governments, organizations, and individuals to effectively adopt, manage, and innovate with new technologies. Closing this gap demands sustained investment in education, vocational training, and professional development programs designed to build digital competencies from primary education through adult reskilling.

Fourth, regional integration emerges as one of the strongest multipliers for ICT progress. Institutions like the Organization of Eastern Caribbean States (OECS) and the Caribbean Community (CARICOM) demonstrate that pooling resources, harmonizing policies, and coordinating initiatives allow small island states to achieve economies of scale and technical sophistication that would be unattainable individually. This regional collaboration enhances purchasing power, fosters shared innovation, and promotes coherent digital governance across member states, amplifying impact and resilience.

Fifth, resilience must be considered a non-negotiable element in ICT infrastructure and strategy. The Eastern Caribbean is vulnerable to natural disasters such as hurricanes, alongside growing cyber threats and economic volatility. ICT systems must be designed with robustness, rapid recovery capabilities, and adaptability to withstand and respond swiftly to crises. This includes disaster-proof physical infrastructure, secure networks, redundant data backups, and flexible governance structures that can pivot as challenges evolve.

Building on these lessons, several actionable recommendations emerge for stakeholders seeking to accelerate and sustain ICT integration in the region. Governments and regional bodies should prioritize establishing unified regional ICT implementation frameworks aligned with internationally recognized standards like the Project Management Body of Knowledge (PMBOK). Such frameworks promote best practices in planning, execution, risk management, and monitoring, reducing the prevalence of fragmented or ad hoc approaches.

Continuous investment in digital literacy programs must become a cornerstone, starting from primary education and extending through lifelong learning and professional reskilling initiatives. This will empower citizens and the workforce to confidently engage with evolving technologies and services.

Creating public-private innovation labs and accelerators can stimulate applied research, development, and adoption of cutting-edge technologies such as blockchain, artificial intelligence, and the Internet of Things (IoT). These hubs would serve as collaborative spaces where government, academia, industry, and startups jointly develop contextually relevant solutions.

Strengthening cybersecurity legislation, regulatory enforcement, and public awareness campaigns is vital to building citizen trust and safeguarding digital ecosystems. Comprehensive cyber laws and proactive governance structures will help protect data privacy and system integrity against emerging threats.

Pursuing regional initiatives to develop cross-border data centers and shared cloud infrastructure also offers opportunities for greater efficiency, cost reduction, and operational resilience. Such efforts can facilitate seamless data sharing, improve service uptime, and enhance disaster recovery capabilities.

By institutionalizing these recommendations through policy frameworks, capacity-building, and sustained multi-stakeholder collaboration, the Eastern Caribbean stands to break free from the costly cycle of failed ICT projects. These efforts will lay the foundation for a sustainable, inclusive, and resilient digital ecosystem capable of driving socio-economic transformation and regional integration in the digital era.

The Role of IT Project Managers as Change Agents

One of the most powerful insights emerging from the research is the pivotal and multifaceted role that IT project managers play in driving digital transformation across the Eastern Caribbean. These individuals are far more than mere technical coordinators or administrators responsible for schedules and budgets; rather, they function as dynamic change agents who bridge the critical gap between visionary strategies and on-the-ground execution. Their impact extends across organizational boundaries and deeply influences the success or failure of ICT initiatives in a region marked by limited resources and complex socio-economic challenges.

The thesis demonstrated that successful project managers exhibit a comprehensive skill set and strategic mindset that goes well beyond conventional project management tasks. They actively translate high-level policy goals and national development agendas into actionable ICT investments and practical implementation plans. In doing so, they ensure that technology deployments are not isolated efforts but integral components of broader developmental objectives such as education reform, public service enhancement, economic diversification, and social inclusion.

Moreover, these managers are adept facilitators of collaboration, navigating complex networks that span government ministries, private sector partners, civil society organizations, and community stakeholders. By fostering open communication and coordination across these diverse actors, they help overcome institutional silos and promote shared ownership of digital projects. Such collaboration is vital in the Caribbean context where collective efforts are often necessary to maximize scarce resources and address interrelated regional challenges.

A critical dimension of their role involves actively promoting user acceptance and adoption of ICT solutions. Project managers apply theoretical frameworks such as the Technology Acceptance Model (TAM) to assess and improve users' perceptions of system usefulness and ease of use. This user-centered approach helps address resistance to change, tailor training and support programs, and ultimately increase the likelihood of sustained engagement with new digital tools. Recognizing that technology is only as effective as its adoption by intended beneficiaries, project managers make acceptance a strategic priority.

Building resilience into ICT systems and projects is another hallmark of effective project management in this region. The Eastern Caribbean faces frequent hurricanes, economic volatility, and mounting cyber threats, all of which can disrupt digital services with far-reaching consequences. Project managers are responsible for embedding contingency planning, disaster recovery strategies, and cybersecurity protocols into project designs, ensuring that critical ICT infrastructure remains robust, adaptable, and capable of maintaining continuity under adverse conditions. This proactive stance on risk mitigation is essential for protecting investments and safeguarding public trust.

Furthermore, successful project managers play a key role in talent development by mentoring and upskilling their teams. Given the region's existing capacity gaps in specialized ICT areas, cultivating a pipeline of qualified local professionals is crucial. Through continuous training, knowledge transfer, and leadership development, project managers help build the human capital necessary for sustaining and evolving the region's digital ecosystem over time.

To fulfill their complex mandate effectively, project managers in the Eastern Caribbean must cultivate a balanced blend of technical expertise and soft skills. Communication, negotiation, cultural sensitivity, and adaptive leadership are just as indispensable as proficiency in project management methodologies and ICT tools. In an environment where resources are constrained and risks are high, these interpersonal and strategic capabilities often determine whether ICT projects achieve measurable social impact or become unrealized ambitions relegated to reports and plans.

Looking ahead, it is imperative that regional institutions—including governments, professional bodies, and educational institutions—invest systematically in the empowerment of this crucial cadre of professionals. Establishing certification programs tailored to the Caribbean context can standardize and elevate project management practices. Creating peer-learning networks will facilitate knowledge exchange and mutual support among practitioners confronting similar challenges. Leadership development initiatives focusing on the unique regional socio-cultural and technological landscape can further prepare managers to lead complex digital transformation ventures effectively.

By prioritizing these capacity-building efforts, the Eastern Caribbean can accelerate its digital journey while ensuring that this progress is inclusive, resilient, and sustainable. Empowered and skilled project managers will serve as catalysts for innovation, champions of collaboration, and guardians of community-centered development—roles essential for translating technological potential into real-world benefits for the diverse peoples of the region.

Vision for the Eastern Caribbean's Digital Future

The digital future of the Eastern Caribbean transcends the mere adoption of new technologies; it encompasses a broader and deeper vision centered on resilience,

328

empowerment, and the affirmation of cultural identity. As small island states navigating an increasingly complex global landscape, these nations cannot realistically compete with the sheer scale and resources of technology giants such as the United States, China, or India. However, the Eastern Caribbean can—and must—lead in areas where agility, creativity, and human-centered innovation offer distinctive advantages. This requires a bold, regionally coherent vision that aligns technological progress with the unique socio-economic realities and cultural strengths of the Caribbean.

At the heart of this vision is the creation of a digitally integrated regional economy. Seamless cross-border transactions, efficient logistics, and vibrant e-commerce ecosystems are essential to unleashing the full potential of interconnected island markets. Initiatives such as DCash, the world's first blockchain-based digital currency union-wide, serve as foundational platforms that facilitate rapid, secure, and cost-effective payments across islands. Building on such innovations, the region can develop blockchain-enabled trade hubs that simplify customs processes, enhance supply chain transparency, and reduce the friction traditionally associated with inter-island commerce. This integrated digital economy will not only boost economic growth but also reduce barriers to market entry for small businesses and entrepreneurs, enabling them to compete on a global scale.

Another pillar of the digital future envisions smart, resilient communities that harness technology to mitigate the region's vulnerabilities—particularly to natural disasters and climate change. Early-warning systems powered by real-time data analytics and sensor networks can provide timely alerts for hurricanes, floods, and other emergencies, enabling more effective evacuation and response. Renewable energy grids managed through ICT provide sustainable power solutions essential to reducing carbon footprints and ensuring energy security. ICT-enabled disaster response networks that integrate government agencies, civil society, and citizens empower communities to respond collectively, minimizing impact and accelerating recovery. By embedding resilience into the very fabric of technological infrastructure, the Eastern Caribbean can safeguard lives, livelihoods, and development gains against future shocks.

The transformation also includes nurturing globally competitive creative industries that leverage emerging technologies such as generative AI, virtual and augmented reality, and digital storytelling. These tools can amplify the unique cultural heritage, music, art, and narratives of the Caribbean, producing immersive virtual tourism experiences and digital content that resonate with audiences worldwide. By marrying technology with Caribbean creativity, the region can generate new streams of income, attract international investment, and project a vibrant cultural identity on the global stage. This approach not only promotes economic diversity but also preserves and reinvigorates traditions in a rapidly digitalizing world.

Education forms a cornerstone of this digital vision. The Eastern Caribbean can develop inclusive education ecosystems that utilize online learning platforms, AI tutors, and regional e-universities to democratize access to high-quality education. Regardless of geographic location or socio-economic status, learners would have the opportunity to engage with world-class curricula tailored to regional needs. This will be critical for addressing the dispersed and uneven distribution of educational resources across the islands. Additionally, such ecosystems support lifelong learning and continuous skills development, preparing citizens for evolving labor market demands in the digital economy.

To sustain innovation momentum, cultivating a vibrant culture of entrepreneurship is vital. The region can foster this by establishing incubators, accelerators, and regional venture capital networks that nurture start-ups and creative enterprises focused on digital products and services. These support mechanisms provide not only funding but also mentorship, market access, and technical assistance, helping innovators translate ideas into viable businesses that contribute to economic resilience and job creation.

Crucially, this bold vision must be deeply rooted in Caribbean values that emphasize community, sustainability, and cultural identity. The purpose of digital transformation is not merely technological advancement for its own sake but the intentional use of technology to enhance human dignity, promote democratic participation, and protect the natural environment. This values-driven approach ensures that technological progress is inclusive, ethical, and aligned with the long-term well-being of Caribbean peoples and ecosystems.

For this vision to be realized, governments, private sector actors, academia, and civil society across the region must embrace a shared commitment and collaborative spirit. By working together through regional institutions and partnerships, the Eastern Caribbean can chart a forward-looking path where ICT becomes much more than a survival mechanism—it becomes a powerful engine of global leadership in ethical, sustainable, and people-centered digital futures. In doing so, the region can transform its unique challenges into opportunities, showcasing how small island states can pioneer innovative models of resilient and culturally grounded digital development in the 21st century.

www.ingramcontent.com/pod-product-compliance
Lightning Source LLC
Chambersburg PA
CBHW040752220326
41597CB00029BA/4741